Ancient Rome

GAIUS JULIUS CAESAR

Ancient Rome
The Great Men, Army and Wars

Robert F. Pennell

LEONAUR

Ancient Rome
The Great Men, Army and Wars
by Robert F. Pennell

First published under the title
Ancient Rome

Leonaur is an imprint of Oakpast Ltd

Copyright in this form © 2011 Oakpast Ltd

ISBN: 978-0-85706-569-8 (hardcover)
ISBN: 978-0-85706-570-4 (softcover)

http://www.leonaur.com

Contents

Preface

This compilation is designed to be a companion to the author's *History of Greece*. It is hoped that it may fill a want, now felt in many high schools and academies, of a short and clear statement of the rise and fall of Rome, with a biography of her chief men, and an outline of her institutions, manners, and religion.

For this new edition the book has been entirely rewritten, additional matter having been introduced whenever it has been found necessary to meet recent requirements.

The maps and plans have been specially drawn and engraved for this book. The design has been to make them as clear and open as possible; consequently, names and places not mentioned in the text have, as a rule, been omitted.

Robert F. Pennell.

Riverside, California,
July, 1890.

CHAPTER 1

Geography of Italy

Italy is a long, narrow peninsula in the southern part of Europe, between the 38th and 46th parallels of north latitude. It is 720 miles long from the Alps to its southern extremity, and 330 miles broad in its widest part, *i. e.* from the Little St. Bernard to the hills north of Trieste. It has an area of nearly 110,000 square miles, about that of the State of Nevada.

The Alps separate Italy on the north and northwest from the rest of Europe. The pass over these mountains which presents the least difficulties is through the Julian Alps on the east It was over this pass that the Barbarians swept down in their invasions of the country. The Apennines, which are a continuation of the Alps, extend through the whole of the peninsula. Starting in the Maritime Alps, they extend easterly towards the Adriatic coast, and turn south-easterly hugging the coast through its whole extent. This conformation of the country causes the rivers of any size below the basin of the Po to flow into the Tyrrhenian (Tuscan) Sea, rather than into the Adriatic.

Northern Italy, between the Alps and the Apennines, is drained by the Padus (Po) and its Tribútaries. It was called **Gallia Cisalpína** (Gaul this side of the Alps), and corresponds in general to modern Lombardy. The little River Athesis, north of the Padus, flows into the Adriatic. Of the Tribútaries of the Padus, the Ticínus on the north, and the Trebia on the south, are of historical interest.

The portion of Northern Italy bordering on the Mediterranean is a mountainous district, and was called **Liguria**. In this district on the coast were Genua and Nicaea. The district north of the Athesis, between the Alps and the Adriatic, was called **Venetia**, from which comes the name Venice. Here were located Patavium (Padua), Aquileia, and Forum Julii.

ANCIENT ITALY

SCALE OF STATUTE MILES

Longitude   West   12   from   Greenwich   16

Latitude markings: 44 · 16 · 12 · 8 · 46 · 42

ADRIATIC SEA

DALMATIA

LIBURNIA

PANNONIA

NORICUM

RHÆTIA

GALLIA CISALPINA

PICENUM

ROME LATIUM

CAMPANIA

ETRURIA

Gulf of Genua

CORSICA

CAPRARIA

ILVA

Aquileia

Verona

Patavium

Andes

Ateste

Mantua

Cremona

Mutina

Placentia

Parma

Tanus R.

Mediolanum

Eporedia

Derthona

Nicæa

Ravenna

Rubicon R.

Ariminum

Metaurus R.

Sena R.

Ancona

Asculum

Aufidus R.

Clitumnus

Thrasymene L.

Perusia

Volaterræ

Arretium

Pisæ

Telamon

IGILIUM

Aleria

CALABRIA
Brundisium
Tarentum
Heraclea
Sybaris
Croton
Locri
Episephyrii
IONIAN SEA
STROMBOLE
Lipari
Mylae
Tyndaris
Messana
Etna
Catana
Enna
Leontini
Gela
Camarina
Panormus
Thermae
Agrigentum
Ecnomus
Selinus
Lilybaeum
Drepanum
AEGATES IS.
MEDITERRANEAN SEA
TYRRHENIAN SEA
Cumae
Cupra
Hadrumetum
Leptis
Thapsus
Utica
CARTHAGE
Tunis
Zama
AFRICA
SARDINIA

Gallia Cisalpína contained many flourishing towns. North of the Padus were Veróna, Mediolánum (Milan), Cremóna, Mantua, Andes, and Vercellae, a noted battlefield. South of this river were Augusta Taurinórum (Turin), Placentia, Parma, Mutina, and Ravenna. The Rubicon, a little stream flowing into the Adriatic, bounded Gallia Cisalpína on the southeast. The Mucra, another little stream, was the southern boundary on the other side of Italy.

Central Italy, *Italia Propria*, or Italy Proper, included all the peninsula below these rivers as far down as Apulia and Lucania. In this division are the Rivers Tiber, Arnus, and Volturnus, which empty into the Mediterranean, and the Metaurus, Aesis, and Aternus, which empty into the Adriatic.

The most important subdivision of Central Italy was **Latium**, bordering on the Tyrrhenian Sea. North of it on the same coast was **Etruria**, and to the south was **Campania**. On the Adriatic coast were **Umbria**, **Picénum**, and **Samnium**.

The cities of Latium were Rome, on the Tiber, and its seaport, Ostia, near the mouth of the same river. Ten miles northwest of Rome was Veii, an Etruscan city, and about the same distance southeast was Alba Longa. Nearly the same distance directly south of Rome, on the coast, was Lavinium, and east-northeast of Rome was Tibur. Neighbouring to Alba Longa were Tusculum and the Alban Lake. The Pomptine Marshes were near the coast, in the southern part of Latium. Lake Regillus was near Rome.

In Etruria were Florentia, Faesulae, Pisae, Arretium, Volaterrae, Clusium, and Tarquinii; also Lake Trasiménus. In Campania were Capua, Neapolis (Naples), Cumae, Baiae, a watering place, Herculaneum, Pompeii, Caudium, Salernum, Casilínum, and Nola. The famous volcano of Vesuvius was here, and also Lake Avernus.

In Umbria, on the coast, were Ariminum and Pisaurum; in the interior were Sentínum and Camerínum. The River Metaurus, noted for the defeat of Hasdrubal, was likewise in Umbria.

In Picenum was Ancóna. In Samnium were Cures and Beneventum.

Southern Italy included **Apulia** and **Calabria** on the Adriatic, **Lucania** and **Bruttium** on the Tyrrhenian Sea.

Apulia is the most level of the countries south of the Rubicon. Its only stream is the Aufidus, on the bank of which at Cannae was fought a famous battle. Arpi, Asculum, and Canusium are interior towns.

In Calabria (or Iapygia) were the cities of Brundisium and Tarentum.

The chief towns in Lucania and Bruttium were settled by the Greeks. Among them were Heacléa, Metapontum, Sybaris, and Thurii, in Lucania; and Croton, Locri, and Rhegium, in Bruttium.

The islands near Italy were important. **Sicily**, with an area of about 10,000 square miles, and triangular in shape, was often called by the poets **Trinacria** (with three promontories). The island contained many important cities, most of which were of Greek origin. Among these were Syracuse, Agrigentum, Messána, Catana, Camarína, Gela, Selínus, Egesta (or Segesta), Panormus, Leontíni, and Enna. There are many mountains, the chief of which is Aetna.

Sardinia is nearly as large as Sicily. **Corsica** is considerably smaller. **Ilva** (Elba) is between Corsica and the mainland. **Igilium** is off Etruria; **Capreae** is in the Bay of Naples; **Strongyle** (Strombóli) and **Lipara** are north of Sicily, and the **Aegátes Insulae** are west of it

CHAPTER 2

The Early Inhabitants of Italy

So far as we know, the early inhabitants of Italy were divided into three races, the **Iapygian**, **Etruscan**, and **Italian**. The **Iapygians** were the first to settle in Italy. They probably came from the north, and were pushed south by later immigrations, until they were crowded into the south-eastern corner of the peninsula (Calabria). Here they were mostly absorbed by the Greeks, who settled in the eighth and seventh centuries all along the southern and south-western coast, and who were more highly civilized. Besides the Iapygians, and distinct from the Etruscans and Italians, were the Venetians and the Ligurians, the former of whom settled in Venetia, the latter in Liguria.

The **Etruscans** at the time when Roman history begins were a powerful and warlike race, superior to the Italians in civilization and the arts of life. They probably came from the north, and at first settled in the plain of the Po; but being afterwards dislodged by the invading Gauls, they moved farther south, into Etruria. Here they formed a confederation of twelve cities between the Arno and the Tiber. Of these cities the most noted were Volsinii, the head of the confederacy, Veii, Volaterrae, Caere, and Clusium. This people also formed scattering settlements in other parts of Italy, but gained no firm foothold. At one time, in the sixth century, they were in power at Rome. Corsica, too, was at this time under their control. Their commerce was considerable. Many well preserved monuments of their art have been discovered, but no one has yet been able to decipher any of the inscriptions upon them. The power of these people was gradually lessened by the Romans, and after the fall of Veii, in 396, became practically extinct.

The **Italians** were of the same origin as the Hellénes, and belonged to the Aryan race, a people that lived in earliest times possibly in Scandinavia. While the Hellenes were settling in Greece, the Italians entered Italy.

At this time the Italians had made considerable progress in civilization. They understood, in a measure, the art of agriculture; the building of houses; the use of wagons and of boats; of fire in preparing food, and of salt in seasoning it They could make various weapons and ornaments out of copper and silver; husband and wife were recognized, and the people were divided into clans (tribes).

That portion of the Italians known as the **Latins** settled in a plain which is bounded on the east and south by mountains, on the west by the Tyrrhenian Sea, and on the north by the high lands of Etruria.

This plain, called **Latium** (flat country), contains about 700 square miles (one half the size of Rhode Island), with a coast of only fifty miles, and no good harbours. It is watered by two rivers, the Tiber, and its Tribútary, the Anio. Hills rise here and there; as Soracte in the northeast, the promontory of Circeium in the southwest, Janiculum near Rome, and the Alban range farther south. The low lands (modern *Campagna*) were malarious and unhealthy. Hence the first settlements were made on the hills, which also could be easily fortified.

The first town established was **Alba**; around this sprung up other towns, as Lanuvium, Aricia, Tusculum, Tibur, Praeneste, Laurentum, Roma, and Lavinium.

LATIUM

These towns, thirty in number, formed a confederacy, called the **Latin Confederacy**, and chose Alba to be its head. An annual festival was celebrated with great solemnity by the magistrates on the Alban Mount, called the Latin festival. Here all the people assembled and offered sacrifice to their common God, Jupiter (*Latiaris*).

CHAPTER 3

The Romans and
Their Early Government

We have learned the probable origin of the **Latins**; how they settled in Latium, and founded numerous towns. We shall now examine
more particularly that one of the Latin towns which was destined to
outstrip all her sisters in prosperity and power.

Fourteen miles from the mouth of the Tiber, the monotonous level of the plain through which the river flows is broken by a cluster of
hills[1] rising to a considerable height, around one of which, the **Palatine**, first settled a tribe of Latins called **Ramnes**,—a name gradually
changed to **Romans**.

When this settlement was formed is not known. Tradition says in
753. It may have been much earlier. These first settlers of Rome were
possibly a colony from Alba. In the early stages of their history they
united themselves with a Sabine colony that had settled north of them
on the **Quirínal Hill**. The name of **Tities** was given to this new tribe.
A third tribe, named **Luceres**, composed, possibly, of conquered Latins, was afterwards added and settled upon the **Coelian Hill**.

All early communities, to which the Romans were no exception,
were composed of several groups of **Families**. The Romans called
these groups **Gentes**, and a single group was called a **Gens**. All the
members of a *gens* were descended from a common ancestor, after
whom the *gens* received its name.

---

1. The seven hills of historic Rome were the Aventine, Capitoline, Coelian, Esquiline (the highest, 218 feet), Palatine, Quirínal, and Viminal. The Janiculum was
on the other side of the Tiber, and was held by the early Romans as a stronghold
against the Etruscans. It was connected with Rome by a wooden bridge (*Pons
Sublicius*).

The head of each family was called **Pater-familias**, and he had absolute authority [2] over his household, even in the matter of life and death.

The Roman government at first was conducted by these Fathers of the families, with a **King**, elected from their own number, and holding office for life. His duties were to command the army, to perform certain sacrifices (as high priest), and to preside over the assembly of the Fathers of the families, which was called the **Senate**, *i. e.* an assembly of old men (*Senex*).

This body was probably originally composed of all the Fathers of the families, but in historical times it was limited to **three hundred** members, holding life office, and appointed during the regal period by the king. Later the appointment was made by the Consuls, still later by the Censors, and for nearly one hundred years before Christ all persons who had held certain offices were thereby vested with the right of seats in the Senate. Hence, during this later period, the number of Senators was greatly in excess of three hundred. The Senators, when addressed, were called **Patres**, or "Fathers," for they were Fathers of the families.

The Romans, as we saw above, were divided at first into three tribes, *Ramnes*, *Titíes*, and *Luceres*. Each tribe was subdivided into ten districts called **Curiae**, and each *curia* into ten clans called **Gentes** (3 tribes, 30 *curiae*, and 300 *gentes*). Every Roman citizen, therefore, belonged to a particular family, at the head of which was a *pater-familias*; every family belonged to a particular *gens*, named after a common ancestor; every *gens* belonged to a particular *curia*; and every *curia* to a particular *tribe*.

We have learned that in the early government of Rome there was a king, and a senate that advised the king. Besides this, there was an assembly composed of all Roman citizens who could bear arms.[3] This assembly of Roman citizens met, from time to time, in an enclosed space called the **Comitium**, which means a place of gathering or coming together. This was between the Palatine and Quirínal hills near the **Forum**, or market-place. This assembly itself was called the **Comitia Curiáta**, *i. e.* an assembly composed of the 30 *curiae*. This body alone had the power of changing the existing laws; of declaring

---

2. Called *patria potestas*.

3. We must remember that at this time no one was a Roman citizen who did not belong to some family. All other residents were either slaves or had no political rights, *i. e.* had no voice in the government.

war or peace; and of confirming the election of kings made by the senate. The voting in this assembly was taken by each *curia*, and the majority of the *curiae* decided any question.

CHAPTER 4

The Early Growth and Internal History of Rome

The position of Rome was superior to that of the other towns in the Latin Confederacy. Situated on the Tiber, at the head of navigation, she naturally became a commercial centre. Her citizens prospered and grew wealthy, and wealth is power. Her hills were natural strongholds, easily held against a foe. Thus we see that she soon became the most powerful of the Latin cities, and when her interests conflicted with theirs, she had no scruples about conquering any of them and annexing their territory.

Thus Alba was taken during the reign of Tullus Hostilius, and his successor, Ancus Marcius, subdued several cities along the river, and at its mouth founded a colony which was named **Ostia**, the seaport of Rome.

At this time (about 625) the Roman territory (*ager Románus*) comprised nearly 250 square miles, being irregular in shape, but lying mostly along the southern bank of the Tiber and extending about ten or twelve miles from the river. It was not materially increased during the next two centuries.

The original founders of Rome and their direct descendants were called **Patricians**, *i. e.* belonging to the *Patres*, or Fathers of the families. They formed a class distinct from all others, jealously protecting their rights against outsiders.

Attached to the Patricians was a class called **Clients**, who, though free, enjoyed no civil rights, *i. e.* they had no voice in the government, but were bound to assist in every way the Patrician, called **Patron**, to whom they were attached. In return, the latter gave them his support, and, looked after their interests. These clients corresponded somewhat to serfs, worked on the fields of their patrons, and bore the name of the *gens* to which their patron belonged. Their origin is uncertain; but they may have come from foreign towns conquered by the Latins, and whose inhabitants had not been made slaves.

In addition to the clients there were actual slaves, who were the property of their masters, and could be bought or sold at pleasure. Sometimes a slave was freed, and then he was called a **Libertus** (freedman) and became the client of his former master.

As Rome grew into commercial prominence, still another class of people flocked into the city from foreign places, who might be called resident foreigners, corresponding in general to the *Metics* at Athens. Such were many merchants and workmen of all trades. These all were supposed to be under the protection of some patrician who acted as their patron.

These three classes, clients, slaves, and resident foreigners, were all of a different race from the Romans. This should be constantly borne in mind.

We have learned that Rome, as she grew in power, conquered many of the Latin towns, and added their territory to hers. The inhabitants of these towns were of the same race as the Romans, but were not allowed any of their civil rights. Most of them were farmers and peasants. Many of them were wealthy. This class of inhabitants on the *ager Románus,* or in Rome itself, were called **Plebeians** (*Plebs,* multitude). Their very name shows that they must have been numerous. They belonged to no *gens* or *curia,* but were free, and allowed to engage in trade and to own property.

In later times (from about 350) all who were not Patricians or slaves were called Plebeians.

THE ARMY.

Until the time of Servius Tullius (about 550) the army was composed entirely of patricians. It was called a **Legio** (a word meaning *levy*), and numbered three thousand infantry called *milites,* from *mille,* a thousand, one thousand being levied from each tribe. The cavalry numbered three hundred at first, one hundred from each tribe, and was divided into three companies called **Centuries**.

During the reign of Servius the demands of the plebeians, who had now become numerous, for more rights, was met by the so called **Servian** reform of the constitution. Heretofore only the patricians had been required to serve in the army. Now all males were liable to

21

service.

To accomplish this, everyone who was a landowner, provided he owned two acres, was enrolled and ranked according to his property. There were five "Classes" of them. The several classes were divided into 193 sub-divisions called "Centuries," each century representing the same amount of property. In the first class there were forty centuries in active service, composed of men under forty-six, forty centuries of reserve, and eighteen centuries of cavalry.

In the second, third, and fourth classes there were twenty centuries each, ten in active service, and ten in reserve. The fifth class had thirty centuries of soldiers, and five of mechanics, musicians, etc.

The first four ranks of the troops were made up of the infantry from the first class. All were armed with a leather helmet, round shield, breastplate, greaves (leg-pieces), spear, and sword. The fifth rank was composed of the second class, who were armed like the first, without breastplate. The sixth rank was composed of the third class, who had neither breastplate nor greaves. Behind these came the fourth class, armed with spears and darts, and the fifth class, having only slings.

Each soldier of the infantry paid for his own equipments; the cavalry, however, received from the state a horse, and food to keep it.

This new organization of both patricians and plebeians was origi-

CAMPANIA

SCALE OF ENGLISH MILES

nally only for military purposes,—that the army might be increased, and the expenses of keeping it more equitably divided among all the people. But gradually, as the influence of the wealthy plebeians began to be felt, the organisation was found well adapted for political purposes, and all the people were called together to vote under it. It was called the **Comitia Centuriáta**, *i. e.* an assembly of centuries. The place of meeting was on the **Campus Martius**, a plain outside of the city.

In this assembly each century had one vote, and its vote was decided by the majority of its individual voters.

The tendency of this system was to give the wealthy the whole power; for since each century represented the same amount of property, the centuries in the upper or richer classes were much smaller than those in the lower or poorer classes, so that a majority of the centuries might represent a small minority of the people. The majority of the wealthy people at Rome were still patricians, so the assembly was virtually controlled by them. In this assembly magistrates were elected, laws made, war declared, and judgment passed in all criminal cases.

CHAPTER 5

The Dynasty of the Tarquins

Of the seven traditional kings of Rome, the last three were undoubtedly of Etruscan origin, and their reigns left in the city many traces of Etruscan influence. The Etruscans were great builders, and the only buildings of importance that Rome possessed, until a much later period, were erected under this dynasty. The names of these kings are said to have been **Lucius Tarquinius Priscus**, **Servius Tullius**, his son-in-law, and **Lucius Tarquinius Superbus**.

Under the first of these kings were built the fine temple of **Jupiter Capitolínus**, on the Capitoline Hill, and nearby shrines to **Juno** and **Minerva**. This temple to Jupiter was called the **Capitolium**, and from it we get our word It was looked upon as the centre of Roman religion and authority, and at times the Senate was convened in it

During this reign the famous **Cloáca Maxima**, or great sewer intended to drain the Campagna, is also said to have been constructed. This sewer was so well built that it is still used, (as at time of first publication.)

Under the second king of this dynasty, Servius Tullius, the city was surrounded with a wall, which included the Palatine, Quirínal, Coelian, and Aventine hills, and also the Janiculum, which was on the opposite side of the river, and connected with the city by a bridge (*pons sublicius*).

The establishment of the new military organization, mentioned in the previous chapter, was attributed also to this king.

The pupil will notice the similarity between these reforms of Tullius and those of Solon of Athens, who lived about the same time. Thus early was the Greek influence felt at Rome.

During the reign of Tullius a temple in honour of **Díana** was erected on the Aventine, to be used by all the Latin towns.

Tarquinius Superbus added to the **Ager Románus** the territory of the city of **Gabii**, and planted two military colonies, which were afterwards lost. The dynasty of the Tarquins ended with the overthrow of this king, and a Republic was established, which lasted until the death of Julius Caesar.

CHAPTER 6

The Consuls and Tribunes

At the close of the dynasty of the Tarquins, the regal form of government was abolished, and instead of one king who held office for life, two officers, called **Consuls**, were elected annually from the **Patricians**, each of whom possessed supreme power, and acted as a salutary check upon the other; so that neither was likely to abuse his power. This change took place towards the close of the sixth century before Christ.

In times of great emergency a person called **Dictator** might be appointed by one of the Consuls, who should have supreme authority; but his tenure of office never exceeded six months, and he must be a patrician. He exercised his authority chiefly outside of the city walls. It was at this time, about 500, that the **Comitia Centuriáta** came to be the more important assembly, superseding in a great measure the **Comitia Curiáta**.

We must remember that in this assembly all criminal cases were tried, magistrates nominated, and laws adopted or rejected. We must not forget that, since it was on a property basis, it was under the control of the patricians, for the great mass of plebeians were poor. Still there were many wealthy plebeians, and so far the assembly was a gain for this party.

About this time the Senate, which heretofore had consisted solely of Fathers of the families (*Patres*), admitted into its ranks some of the richest of the landed plebeians, and called them **Conscripti**.[1] These, however, could take no part in debates, nor could they hold magistracies.

---

1. This is the origin of the phrase used by speakers addressing the Senate, *viz.*: "*Patres (et) Conscripti.*"

In the Senate, thus constituted, the nomination of all magistrates made in the Comitia Centuriáta was confirmed or rejected. In this way it controlled the election of the Consuls, whose duties, we must remember, were those of generals and supreme judges, though every Roman citizen had the privilege of appealing from their decision in cases which involved life.

Two subordinate officers, chosen from the patricians, were appointed by the Consuls. These officers, called **Quaestóres**, managed the finances of the state, under the direction of the Senate.

The wars in which the Romans had been engaged, during the century preceding the establishment of the Republic, had impoverished the state and crippled its commerce. This was felt by all classes, but especially by the small landed plebeians whose fields had been devastated. They were obliged to mortgage their property to pay the taxes, and, when unable to meet the demands of their creditors, according to the laws they could be imprisoned, or even put to death.

The rich landowners, on the other hand, increased their wealth by "farming" the public revenues; i. e. the state would let out to them, for a stipulated sum, the privilege of collecting all import and other duties. These, in turn (called in later times **Publicans**), would extort all they could from the tax-payers, thus enriching themselves unlawfully. So the hard times, the oppression of the tax-gatherer, and the unjust law about debt, made the condition of the poor unendurable.

The military service, too, bore hard upon them. Many were obliged to serve more than their due time, and in a rank lower than was just; for the Consuls, who had charge of the levy of troops, were patricians, and naturally favoured their own party. Hence we see that the cavalry service was at this time made up entirely of young patricians, while the older ones were in the reserve corps, so that the brunt of military duty fell on the plebeians.

This state of things could not last, and, as the opportunity for rebelling against this unjust and cruel oppression was offered, the plebeians were not slow in accepting it.

The city was at war with the neighbouring Sabines, Aequians, and Volscians, and needed extra men for defence. One of the Consuls liberated all who were confined in prison for debt, and the danger was averted. Upon the return of the army, however, those who had been set free were again thrown into prison. The next year the prisoners were again needed. At first they refused to obey, but were finally persuaded by the Dictator. But after a well-earned victory, upon their return to the city walls, the plebeians of the army deserted, and, marching to a hill nearby, occupied it, threatening to found a new city unless their wrongs were redressed. This is called the **First Secession of the Plebs**, and is said to have been in 494.

The patricians and richer plebeians saw that concessions must be made, for the loss of these people would be ruin to Rome. Those in debt were released from their obligations, and the plebeians received the right to choose annually, from their own numbers, two officers called **Tribúni Plebis**, who should look after their interests, and have the power of **vetoing** any action taken by any magistrate in the city. This power, however, was confined within the city walls, and could never be exercised outside of them.

The person of the Tribunes was also made sacred, to prevent interference with them while in discharge of their duties, and if any one attempted to stop them he was committing a capital crime. Thus, if the Consuls or *Quaestors* were inclined to press the law of debt to extremes, or to be unjust in the levying of troops, the Tribunes could step in, and by their **veto** stop the matter at once.

This was an immense gain for the plebeians, and they were justified in giving the name of **Sacred Mount** to the hill to which they had seceded.

The number of Tribunes was afterwards increased to five, and still later to ten.

CHAPTER 7

The Comitia Tribúta and the Agrarian Laws

The next gain made by the plebeians was the annual appointment from their own ranks of two officers, called **Aediles**.[1] These officers held nearly the same position in reference to the Tribunes that the *Quaestors* did to the Consuls. They assisted the Tribunes in the performance of their various duties, and also had special charge of the temple of Ceres. In this temple were deposited, for safe keeping, all the decrees of the Senate.

These two offices, those of Tribune and Aedile, the result of the first secession, were filled by elections held at first in the Comitia Centuriáta, but later in an assembly called the **Comitia Tribúta**, which met sometimes within and sometimes without the city walls.

This assembly was composed of plebeians, who voted by "tribes" (*tribúta*, meaning composed of tribes), each tribe being entitled to one vote, and its vote being decided by the majority of its individual voters.[2]

The Comitia Tribúta was convened and presided over by the Tribunes and Aediles. In it were discussed matters of interest to the plebeians. By it any member could be punished for misconduct, and though at first measures passed in it were not binding on the people at large, it presently became a determined body, with competent and bold leaders, who were felt to be a power in the state.

The aim of the patricians was now to lessen the power of the

---

1. The word "Aedile" is derived from *Aedes*, meaning temple.
2. These "tribes" were a territorial division, corresponding roughly to "wards" in our cities. At this time there were probably sixteen, but later there were thirty-five. The plebeians in the city lived mostly in one quarter, on the Aventine Hill.

Tribunes; that of the plebeians, to restrain the Consuls and extend the influence of the Tribunes. Party spirit ran high; even hand to hand contests occurred in the city. Many families left Rome and settled in neighbouring places to escape the turmoil. It is a wonder that the government withstood the strain, so fierce was the struggle.

The **Agrarian Laws** at this time first become prominent. These laws had reference to the distribution of the **Public Lands**. Rome had acquired a large amount of land taken from the territory of conquered cities. This land was called **Ager Publicus**, or *public land*.

Some of this land was sold or given away as "homesteads," and then it became **Ager Privátus**, or *private land*. But the most of it was occupied by permission of the magistrates. The occupants were usually rich patricians, who were favoured by the patrician magistrates. This land, so occupied, was called **Ager Occupátus**, or *possessio*; but it really was still the property of the state. The rent paid was a certain *per cent* (from 10 to 20) of the crops, or so much a head for cattle on pasture land. Although the state had the undoubted right to claim this land at any time, the magistrates allowed the occupants to retain it, and were often lenient about collecting dues. In course of time, this land, which was handed down from father to son, and frequently sold, began to be regarded by the occupants as their own property.

Also the land tax (**tribútum**), which was levied on all *ager privátus*, and which was especially hard upon the small plebeian landowners, could not legally be levied upon the *ager occupátus*. Thus the patricians who possessed, not owned, this land were naturally regarded as usurpers by the plebeians.

The first object of the **Agrarian Laws** was to remedy this evil.

Spurius Cassius, an able man, now came forward (486?), proposing a law that the state take up these lands, divide them into small lots, and distribute them among the poor plebeians as homes (homesteads). The law was carried, but in the troublesome times it cost Cassius his life, and was never enforced.

CHAPTER 8

The Contest of the Plebeians for Civil Rights

The plebeians were now (about 475) as numerous as the patricians, if not more so. Their organization had become perfected, and many of their leaders were persistent in their efforts to better the condition of their followers. Their especial aim was to raise their civil and political rights to an equality with those of the patricians. The struggle finally culminated in the murder of one of the Tribunes, Gnarus Genucius, for attempting to veto some of the acts of the Consuls.

Valero Publilius, a Tribune, now (471) proposed and carried, notwithstanding violent opposition by the patricians, a measure to the effect that the Tribunes should hereafter be chosen in the *Comitia Tribúta*, instead of the *Comitia Centuriáta*. Thus the plebeians gained a very important step. This bill is called the **Publilian Law** (*Plebiscitum* [1] *Publilium*).

For the next twenty years the struggle continued unabated. The plebeians demanded a **written code of laws**.

We find among all early peoples that the laws are at first the un-written ones of custom and precedent. The laws at Rome, thus far, had been interpreted according to the wishes and traditions of the patricians only. A change was demanded. This was obtained by the **Terentilian Rogation**, a proposal made in 461 by Gaius Terentilian Harsa, a Tribune, to the effect that the laws thereafter be written. The patrician families, led by one Kaeso Quinctius, made bitter opposition. Kaeso himself, son of the famous Cincinnátus, was impeached by the

---

1. All bills passed in the *Comitia Tribúta* were called Plebiscíta, and until 286 were not necessarily binding upon the people at large; but this bill seems to have been recognized as a law.

Tribune and fled from the city.

Finally it was arranged that the *Comitia Centuriáta* should select from the people at large ten men, called the **Decemvirate**, to hold office for one year, to direct the government and supersede all other magistrates, and especially to draw up a code of laws to be submitted to the people for approval. A commission of three patricians was sent to Athens to examine the laws of that city, which was now (454) at the height of its prosperity. Two years were spent by this commission, and upon their return in 452 the above mentioned *Decemvirate* was appointed.

The laws drawn up by this board were approved, engraved on ten tables of copper, and placed in the *Forum* in front of the Senate-House. Two more tables were added the next year. These **Twelve Tables** were the only Roman code.

The **Decemviri** should have resigned as soon as these laws were approved, but they neglected to do so, and began to act in a cruel and tyrannical manner. The people, growing uneasy under their injustice, finally rebelled when one of the *Decemviri*, Appius Claudius, passed a sentence that brought an innocent maiden, Virginia, into his power. Her father, Virginius, saved his daughter's honour by stabbing her to the heart, and fleeing to the camp called upon the soldiers to put down such wicked government.

A second time the army deserted its leaders, and seceded to the **Sacred Mount**, where they nominated their own Tribunes. Then, marching into the city, they compelled the *Decemviri* to resign.

The **Twelve Tables** have not been preserved, except in fragments, and we know but little of their exact contents. The position of the debtor was apparently made more endurable. The absolute control of the *pater familias* over his family was abolished. The close connection heretofore existing between the clients and patrons was gradually relaxed, the former became less dependent upon the latter, and finally were absorbed into the body of the plebeians. *Gentes* among the plebeians now began to be recognized; previously only the patricians had been divided into *gentes*.

Thus we see, socially, the two orders were approaching nearer and nearer.

In 449 Valerius and Horatius were elected Consuls, and were instrumental in passing the so called **Valerio-Horatian** laws, the substance of which was as follows:—

1. Every Roman citizen could appeal to the *Comitia Centuriáta* against the sentence of any magistrate.

2. All the decisions of the *Comitia Tribúta* (*plebiscíta*), if sanctioned by the Senate and *Comitia Centuriáta*, were made binding upon patricians and plebeians alike. This assembly now became of equal importance with the other two.

3. The persons of the Tribunes, *Aediles*, and other plebeian officers, were to be considered sacred.

4. The Tribunes could take part in the debates of the Senate, and veto any of its decisions.

Two years later (447), the election of the *Quaestors*, who must still be patricians, was intrusted to the *Comitia Tribúta*. Heretofore they had been appointed by the Consuls.

In 445 the Tribune Canuleius proposed a bill which was passed, and called the **Canuleian Law**, giving to the plebeians the right of intermarriage (*connubium*) with the patricians, and enacting that all issue of such marriages should have the rank of the father.

Canuleius also proposed another bill which he did not carry; *viz.* that the consulship be open to the plebeians. A compromise, however, was made, and it was agreed to suspend for a time the office of Consul, and to elect annually six **Military Tribunes** in the *Comitia Centuriáta*, the office being open to all citizens. The people voted every year whether they should have consuls or military tribunes, and this custom continued for nearly a half-century. The patricians, however, were so influential, that for a long time no plebeian was elected.

As an offset to these gains of the plebeians, the patricians in 435 obtained two new officers, called **Censors**, elected from their own ranks every five years (*lustrum*) to hold office for eighteen months.

The duties of the Censors were:—

1. To see that the citizens of every class were properly registered.

2. To punish immorality in the Senate by the removal of any members who were guilty of offences against public morals.

3. To have the general supervision of the finances and public works of the state. This office became in after years the most coveted at Rome.

A few years later, in 421, the plebeians made another step forward by obtaining the right of electing one of their number as *Quaestor*.

There were now four *Quaestors*.

Thus the patricians, in spite of the most obstinate resistance, sustained loss after loss. Even the rich plebeians, who had hitherto often found it for their interest to side with the patricians, joined the farmers or lower classes.

Finally, in 367, the Tribunes Licinius and Sextius proposed and passed the following bills, called the **Licinian Rogations**.

1. To abolish the six military tribunes, and elect annually, as formerly, two Consuls, choosing one or both of them from the plebeians.

2. To forbid any citizen's holding more than 500 *jugera* (300 acres) of the public lands, or feeding thereon more than 100 oxen or 500 sheep.

3. To compel all landlords to employ on their fields a certain number of free labourers, proportionate to the number of their slaves.

4. To allow all interest hitherto paid on borrowed money to be deducted from the principal, and the rest to be paid in three yearly instalments.

These rogations were a great gain for the poorer classes. It gave them an opportunity for labour which had previously been performed mostly by slaves. They were less burdened by debts, and had some prospect of becoming solvent. But most of all, since the office of Consul was open to them, they felt that their interests were now more likely to be protected. The temple of **Concordia** in the *Forum* was dedicated by Camillus as a mark of gratitude for the better times that these rogations promised.

The plebeians, however, did not stop until all the offices, except that of *Interrex*, were thrown open to them. First they gained that of Dictator, then those of Censor and of *Praetor*, and finally, in 286, by the law of **Hortensius**, the *plebiscíta* became binding upon all the people without the sanction of the Senate and *Comitia Centuriáta*. After 200 the sacred offices of **Pontifex** and **Augur** also could be filled by plebeians.

Thus the strife that had lasted for two centuries was virtually ended; and although the Roman patricians still held aloof from the commons, yet their rights as citizens were no greater than those of the plebeians.

To recapitulate:——

Full citizenship comprised four rights, *viz.*: that of trading and holding property (**commercium**); that of voting (**suffragium**); that of intermarriage (**connubium**); and that of holding office (**honores**).

The first of these rights the plebeians always enjoyed; the second they obtained in the establishment of the **Comitia Tribúta**; the third by the **Canuleian** bill; the fourth by the **Licinian** and subsequent bills.

CHAPTER 9

External History

The first authentic history of Rome begins about 400. The city then possessed, possibly, three hundred square miles of territory. The number of tribes had been increased to twenty-five. Later it became thirty-five.

In 391 a horde of Celtic barbarians crossed the Apennines into Etruria and attacked **Clusium**. Here a Celtic chief was slain by Roman ambassadors, who, contrary to the sacred character of their mission, were fighting in the ranks of the Etrurians. The Celts, in revenge, marched upon Rome. The disastrous Battle of the **Allia**, a small river about eleven miles north of the city, was fought on July 18, 390. The Romans were thoroughly defeated and their city lay at the mercy of the foe. The Celts, however, delayed three days before marching upon Rome. Thus the people had time to prepare the Capitol for a siege, which lasted seven months, when by a large sum of money the barbarians were induced to withdraw.

During this siege the records of the city's history were destroyed, and we have no trustworthy data for events that happened previous to 390.

The city was quickly rebuilt and soon recovered from the blow. In 387 the lost territory adjacent to the Tiber was annexed, and military colonies were planted at Sutrium and Nepete upon the Etruscan border, and also at Circeii and Setia.[1] The neighbouring Latin town

---

1. These military colonies, of which the Romans subsequently planted many, were outposts established to protect conquered territory. A band of Roman citizens was armed and equipped, as if for military purposes. They took with them their wives and children, slaves and followers, and established a local government similar to that of Rome. These colonists relinquished their rights as Roman citizens and became Latins; hence the name **Latin Colonies.**

of **Tusculum**, which had always been a faithful ally, was annexed to Rome.

The trying times of these years had caused numerous enemies to spring up all around Rome; but she showed herself superior to them all, until finally, in 353, she had subdued the whole of Southern Etruria, and gained possession of the town of **Caere**, with most of its territory. The town was made a **Municipium**, the first of its kind.

The inhabitants, being of foreign blood and language, were not allowed the full rights of Roman citizenship, but were permitted to govern their own city in local matters as they wished. Many towns were subsequently made *municipia*. Their inhabitants were called *cives sine suffragio*, "citizens without suffrage."

During the next ten years (353-343) Rome subdued all the lowland countries as far south as **Tarracína**. To the north, across the Tiber, she had acquired most of the territory belonging to **Veii** and **Capéna**.

In 354 she formed her first connections beyond the Liris, by a treaty with the **Samnites**, a race that had established itself in the mountainous districts of Central Italy, This people, spreading over the southern half of Italy, had in 423 captured the Etruscan city of **Capua**, and three years later the Greek city of **Cumae**. Since then they had been practically masters of the whole of Campania.

After the treaty of 354 mentioned above, both the Romans and Samnites had, independently of each other, been waging war upon the Volsci. The Samnites went so far as to attack Teánum, a city of Northern Campania, which appealed to Capua for aid. The Samnites at once appeared before Capua, and she, unable to defend herself, asked aid of Rome.

Alarmed at the advances of the Samnites, Rome only awaited an excuse to break her treaty. This was furnished by the Capuans surrendering their city unconditionally to Rome, so that, in attacking the Samnites, she would simply be defending her subjects.

Thus began the **Samnite Wars**, which lasted for over half a century with varying success, and which were interrupted by two truces. It is usual to divide them into three parts, the First, Second, and Third Samnite Wars.

THE FIRST SAMNITE WAR (343-341).

The accounts of this war are so uncertain and confused that no clear idea of its details can be given. It resulted in no material advantage to either side, except that Rome retained Capua and made it a *municipium*, annexing its territory to her own.

THE LATIN WAR (340-338).

The cities of the **Latin Confederacy** had been for a long time looking with jealous eyes upon the rapid progress of Rome. Their own rights had been disregarded, and they felt that they must now make a stand or lose everything. They sent to Rome a proposition that one of the Consuls and half of the Senate be Latins; but it was rejected. A war followed, in the third year of which was fought the Battle of Trigánum, near Mount Vesuvius. The Romans, with their Samnite allies, were victorious through the efforts of the Consul, **Titus Manlius Torquátus**, one of the illustrious names of this still doubtful period. The remainder of the operations was rather a series of expeditions against individual cities than a general war.

In 338 all the Latins laid down their arms, and the war closed. The Latin confederacy was at an end. Rome now was mistress. Four of the Latin cities, **Tibur**, **Praeneste**, **Cora**, and **Laurentum**, were left independent, but all the rest of the towns were annexed to Rome. Their territory became part of the *Ager Románus*, and the inhabitants Roman plebeians.

Besides acquiring Latium, Rome also annexed, as *municipia*, three more towns, Fundi, Formiae, and Velítrae, a Volscian town.

Latium was now made to include all the country from the Tiber to the Volturnus.

Rome about this time established several **Maritime** (Roman) **Colonies**, which were similar to her **Military** (Latin) **Colonies**, except that the colonists retained all their rights as Roman citizens, whereas the military colonists relinquished these rights and became Latins. The first of these colonies was **Antium** (338); afterwards were established **Tarracína** (329), **Minturnae**, and **Sinuessa** (296). Others were afterwards founded.

Later, when Antium was changed into a military colony, its navy was destroyed, and the beaks (*rostra*) of its ships were taken to Rome, and placed as ornaments on the speaker's stand opposite the Senate-House. Hence the name **Rostra**.

At this time the **Forum**, which had been used for trading purposes of all kinds, was improved and beautified. It became a centre for political discussions and financial proceedings. The bankers and brokers had their offices here. Smaller *Fora* were started near the river, as the *Forum*

Boarium (cattle market) and the *Forum Holitorium* (vegetable market).

Maenius, one of the Censors, was chiefly instrumental in bringing about these improvements.

THE SECOND AND THIRD SAMNITE WARS (326-290).

The results of the First Samnite War and the Latin War were, as we have seen, to break up the Latin confederacy, and enlarge the domain of Rome.

There were now in Italy three races aiming at the supremacy, the **Romans**, the **Samnites**, and the **Etruscans**. The last of these was the weakest, and had been declining ever since the capture by the Romans of Veii in 396, and of Caere in 353.

In the contest which followed between Rome and the Samnites, the combatants were very nearly matched. Rome had her power more compact and concentrated, while the Samnites were superior in numbers., but were more scattered. They were both equally brave.

During the first five years of the war (326-321), the Romans were usually successful, and the Samnites were forced to sue for peace. In this period Rome gained no new territory, but founded a number of military posts in the enemy's country.

The peace lasted for about a year, when hostilities were again renewed. By this time the Samnites had found a worthy leader in **Gavius Pontius**, by whose skill and wisdom the fortune of war was turned against the Romans for seven years (321-315). He allured the Romans into a small plain, at each end of which was a defile (**Furculae Caudínae**). On reaching this plain they found Pontius strongly posted to oppose them. After a bloody but fruitless attempt to force him to retreat, the Romans themselves were compelled to give way. But meanwhile Pontius had also occupied the defile in their rear, and they were obliged to surrender.

A treaty was signed by the Consuls Titus Veturius and Spurius Postumius, according to which peace was to be made, and everything restored to its former condition.

Such was the affair at the **Caudine Forks** (321), one of the most humiliating defeats that ever befell the Roman arms. The army was made to pass under the yoke,—which was made of three spears, two stuck into the ground parallel to each other and the third placed above them,—and then suffered to depart.

Rome was filled with dismay at the news. The citizens dressed in mourning, business and amusements were suspended, and every energy was devoted to repairing the disaster. Compliance with the terms of the treaty was refused, on the ground that no treaty was valid unless sanctioned by a vote of the people. It was determined to deliver the Consuls who had signed it to the enemy.

Pontius, indignant at the broken faith, refused to accept them, and the war was renewed. It continued for seven years, when (310) the Samnites were so thoroughly whipped by **Quintus Fabius**, then Dictator, at **Lake Vadimónis** in Etruria, that they could no longer make any effective resistance, and at last (304) agreed to relinquish all their sea-coast, their alliances and conquests, and acknowledge the supremacy of Rome.

During this war the Etruscans made their last single effort against the Roman power. An expedition was sent in 311 to attack the military colony of Sutrium, which had been founded seventy-six years before. The Consul Quintus Fabius went to the rescue, raised the siege, drove the Etruscans into the Ciminian forests, and there completely defeated them.

Six years intervened between the Second and the **Third Samnite War** (298-290). This time was employed by the Samnites in endeavouring to unite Italy against Rome. They were joined by the **Umbrians, Gauls**, and **Etruscans**. The **Lucanians** alone were with Rome.

The war was of short duration, and was practically decided by the sanguinary Battle of **Sentínum** (295) in Umbria. The Samnites, led by Gellius Egnatius, were routed by the Roman Consuls **Quintus Fabius Maximus** and **Publius Decius Mus**.

In this battle the struggle was long and doubtful. The Samnites were assisted by the Gauls, who were showing themselves more than a match for the part of the Roman army opposed to them, and commanded by Decius. Following the example of his illustrious father, the Consul vowed his life to the Infernal Gods if victory were granted, and, rushing into the midst of the enemy, was slain.[2] His soldiers, rendered enthusiastic by his example, rallied and pushed back the Gauls. The victory was now complete, for the Samnites were already fleeing before that part of the army which was under Fabius.

The war dragged on for five years, when the Consul **Manius Curius Dentátus** finally crushed the Samnites, and also the **Sabines**, who had recently joined them. The Samnites were allowed their independence, and became allies of Rome. The Sabines were made Ro-

---

2. It is said that the father of Decius acted in a similar manner in a battle of the Latin war.

man citizens (*sine suffragio*), and their territory was annexed to the *Ager Románus*. This territory now reached across Italy from the Tuscan to the Adriatic Sea, separating the Samnites and other nations on the south from the Umbrians, Gauls, and Etruscans on the north.

In 283, at Lake Vadimónis, the Romans defeated the Senonian and Boian Gauls, and founded the military colony of **Sena Gallica**.

CHAPTER 10

Wars with Pyrrhus (281-272)

In the early times of Rome, while she was but little known, it had been the custom of Greece to send colonies away to relieve the pressure of too rapid increase. We find them in Spain, France, Asia Minor, and especially in Sicily and Southern Italy, where the country became so thoroughly Grecianized that it was called **Magna Graecia**. Here were many flourishing cities, as Tarentum, Sybaris, Croton, and Thurii. These had, at the time of their contact with Rome, greatly fallen from their former grandeur, owing partly to the inroads of barbarians from the north, partly to civil dissensions, and still more to their jealousy of each other; so that they were unable to oppose any firm and united resistance to the progress of Rome. It had been their custom to rely largely upon strangers for the recruiting and management of their armies,—a fact which explains in part the ease with which they were overcome.

Of these cities **Tarentum** was now the chief. With it a treaty had been made by which the Tarentines agreed to certain limits beyond which their fleet was not to pass, and the Romans bound themselves not to allow their vessels to appear in the Gulf of Tarentum beyond the Lacinian promontory. As usual, the Romans found no difficulty in evading their treaty whenever it should profit them.

Thurii was attacked by the Lucanians, and, despairing of aid from Tarentum, called on Rome for assistance. As soon as domestic affairs permitted, war was declared against the Lucanians, and the wedge was entered which was to separate Magna Graecia from Hellas, and deliver the former over to Rome.

Pretending that the war was instigated by Tarentum, Rome decided to ignore the treaty, and sent a fleet of ten vessels into the Bay of Tarentum. It was a gala day, and the people were assembled in the theatre that overlooked the bay when the ships appeared. It was determined to punish the intrusion. A fleet was manned, and four of the Roman squadron were destroyed.

An ambassador, Postumius, sent by Rome to demand satisfaction, was treated with insult and contempt. He replied to the mockery of the Tarentines, that their blood should wash out the stain. The next year one of the Consuls was ordered south.

Meanwhile Tarentum had sent envoys to ask aid of **Pyrrhus**, the young and ambitious **King of Epírus**. He was cousin of Alexander the Great, and, since he had obtained no share in the division of the conquests of this great leader, his dream was to found an empire in the West that would surpass the exhausted monarchies of the East.

Pyrrhus landed in Italy in 281 with a force of 20,000 infantry, 3,000 cavalry, and 20 elephants. He at once set about compelling the effeminate Greeks to prepare for their own defence. Places of amusement were closed; the people were forced to perform military duty; disturbers of the public safety were put to death; and other reforms were made which the dangers of the situation seemed to demand.

Meanwhile the Romans acted with promptness, and boldly challenged him to battle. The armies met in 280 on the plain of **Heracléa**, on the banks of the Liris, where the level nature of the country was in favour of the Greek method of fighting. The Macedonian *phalanx* was the most perfect instrument of warfare the world had yet seen, and the Roman legions had never yet been brought into collision with it.

The Romans, under **Laevínus**, were defeated, more by the surprise of a charge of elephants than by the tactics of the phalanx. However, they retired in good order. Pyrrhus is said to have been much impressed by the heroic conduct of the foe, and to have said, " Another such victory will send me back without a man to Epirus." He recognized the inferior qualities of his Greek allies, and determined to make a peace. A trusted messenger, **Cineas**, was sent to Rome. He was noted for his eloquence, which was said to have gained more for his master than the sword. Through him Pyrrhus promised to retire to Epirus if safety was guaranteed to his allies in Italy.

The eloquence of Cineas was fortified with presents for the Senators; and though these were refused, many seemed disposed to treat with him, when the aged **Appius Claudius Caecus** (Blind) was led into the Senate, and declared that Rome should never treat with an enemy in arms.

Cineas was deeply impressed by the dignity of the Romans, and declared that the Senators were an assembly of kings and Rome itself a temple.

Pyrrhus then tried force, and, hastily advancing northward, appeared within eighteen miles of the city. Here his danger became great. The defection he had hoped for among the Latins did not take place, and the armies which had been operating elsewhere were now ready to unite against him. He therefore retired into winter quarters at Tarentum, where he received the famous embassy of **Gaius Fabricius**, sent to propose an interchange of prisoners. It was in vain that bribes and threats were employed to shake the courage of the men sent by the Senate; and, on his part, Pyrrhus refused to grant the desired exchange.

Many Italian nations now joined Pyrrhus, and hostilities were renewed. The armies again met in 279 on the plain of **Asculum**, in Apulia; but though the Romans were defeated, it was only another of those Pyrrhic victories which were almost as disastrous as defeat

The same year Pyrrhus retired to Sicily to defend Syracuse against the Carthaginians, who were allied to the Romans. He remained on the island three years. Upon his return to Italy he met the Romans for the last time in 274, near **Beneventum**, where he was defeated by the Consul **Manius Curius Dentátus**. The Romans had by this time become accustomed to the elephants, and used burning arrows against them. The wounded beasts became furious and unmanageable, and threw the army into disorder. With this battle ended the career of Pyrrhus in Italy. He returned home, and two years later was accidentally killed by a woman at Argos.

The departure of Pyrrhus left all Italy at the mercy of Rome. Two years later, in 272, the garrison at Tarentum surrendered, the city walls were demolished, and the fleet given up.

CHAPTER 11

Divisions of the Roman Territory— Noted Men of the Period

Rome was now mistress of all Italy south of the Arnus and Aesis. This country was divided into two parts,

1. The **Ager Románus**, including about one quarter of the whole, bounded on the north by **Caere**, on the south by **Formiae**, and on the east by the **Apennines**.

2. The **Dependent Communities**.

The *Ager Románus* was subdivided, for voting and financial purposes, into thirty-three, afterwards thirty-five districts (tribes), four of which were in Rome. The elections were all held at Rome.

These districts were made up,—

a. Of **Rome**.

b. Of the **Roman Colonies**, mostly maritime, now numbering seven, but finally increased to thirty-five.

c. Of the **Municipia** (towns bound to service).

d. Of the **Praefectúrae** (towns governed by a *praefect*, who was sent from Rome and appointed by the *Praetor*). The Dependent Communities were made up,—

> *a.* Of the **Latin** (military) **Colonies**, now numbering twenty-two, afterwards increased to thirty-five.

> *b.* Of the **Allies** of Rome (*Socii*), whose cities and adjoining territory composed more than one half of the country controlled by Rome.

> These allies were allowed local government, were not

obliged to pay tribute, but were called upon to furnish their proportion of troops for the Roman army.

The inhabitants of this country were divided into **five** classes, viz.:—

a. Those who possessed both **Public** and **Private Rights** as citizens, *i. e.* **Full Rights**. [1]

b. Those who were subjects and did not possess full rights.

c. Those who were **Allies** (*Socii*).

d. Those who were **Slaves**, who possessed no rights.

e. Those who were **Resident Foreigners**, who possessed the right of trading.

To class *a* belonged the citizens of Rome, of the Roman colonies, and of some of the Municipia.

To class *b* belonged the citizens of most of the Municipia, who possessed only private rights, the citizens of all the *Praefectúrae* y and the citizens of all the Latin colonies.

ROADS.

Even at this early date, the necessity of easy communication with the capital seems to have been well understood. Roads were pushed in every direction,—broad, level ways, over which armies might be marched or intelligence quickly carried. They were chains which bound her possessions indissolubly together. Some of them remain to-day a monument of Roman thoroughness, enterprise, and sagacity,—the wonder and admiration of modern road-builders. By these means did Rome fasten together the constantly increasing fabric of her empire, so that not even the successes of Hannibal caused more than a momentary shaking of fidelity, for which ample punishment was both speedy and certain.

NOTED MEN.

The three most noted men of the period embraced in the two preceding chapters were Appius Claudius, the Censor and patrician;

---

1. Public rights consisted of the *jus suffragii* (right of voting at Rome); *jus honórum* (right of holding office) , and *jus provocatiónis* (right of appeal). Private rights were *jus connubii* (right of intermarriage); and *jus commercii* (right of trading and holding property). Full rights were acquired either by birth or gift. A child born of parents, both of whom enjoyed the *jus connubii*, was a Roman citizen with full rights. Foreigners were sometimes presented with citizenship (*civitas*).

and Manius Curius Dentátus and Gaius Fabricius, plebeians.

We have seen that all plebeians who were landowners belonged to one of the tribes, and could vote in the *Comitia Tribúta*; this, however, shut out the plebeians of the city who owned no land, and also the freedmen, who were generally educated and professional men, such as doctors, teachers, etc.

Appius Claudius as Censor, in 312, deprived the land-owners of the exclusive privilege of voting in the *Comitia Tribúta*, and gave to property owners of any sort the right to vote. Eight years later this law was modified, so that it applied to the four city tribes alone, and the thirty-one rural tribes had for their basis landed property only.

During the censorship of Appius, Rome had its first regular water supply by the Appian aqueduct. The first military road, the **Via Appia**, was built under his supervision. This road ran at first from Rome as far as Capua. It was constructed so well that many parts of it are today in good condition. The road was afterward extended to Brundisium, through Venusia and Tarentum.

Manius Curius Dentátus was a peasant, a contemporary of Appius, and his opponent in many ways. He was a strong friend of the plebeians. He obtained for the soldiers large assignments of the *Ager Publicus*. He drained the low and swampy country near Reáte by a canal. He was the conqueror of Pyrrhus. A man of sterling qualities, frugal and unostentatious, after his public life he retired to his farm and spent the remainder of his days in seclusion as a simple peasant.

Gaius Fabricius, like Dentátus, was from the peasants. He was a Hernican. As a soldier he was successful. As a statesman he was incorruptible, and of great use to his country. Previous to the battle of Asculum, Pyrrhus attempted to bribe him by large sums of money, and, failing in this, thought to frighten him by hiding an elephant behind a curtain; the curtain was suddenly removed, but Fabricius, though immediately under the elephant's trunk, stood unmoved.

In this generation we find Roman character at its best. Wealth had not flowed into the state in such large quantities as to corrupt it. The great mass of the people were peasants, small landowners, of frugal habits and moral qualities. But comparatively few owned large estates as yet, or possessed large tracts of the *Ager Publicus*. A century later, when most of the available land in the peninsula was held by the wealthy and farmed by slaves, we find a great change.

The fall of **Tarentum** marks an important era in Roman history. Large treasures were obtained from this and other Greek cities in Southern Italy. Luxury became more fashionable; morals began to degenerate. Greed for wealth obtained by plunder began to get possession of the Romans. From now on the moral tone of the people continued to degenerate in proportion as their empire increased.

CHAPTER 12

Rome and Carthage— First Punic War (264-241)

While Rome was gradually enlarging her territory from Latium to the Straits of Messána, on the other shore of the Mediterranean, opposite Italy and less than one hundred miles from Sicily, sprang up, through industry and commerce, the Carthaginian power.

Like Rome, Carthage had an obscure beginning. As in the case of Rome, it required centuries to gain her power.

It was the policy of Carthage to make a successful revolt of her subdued allies an impossibility, by consuming all their energies in the support of her immense population and the equipment of her numerous fleets and armies. Hence all the surrounding tribes, once wandering nomads, were forced to become tillers of the soil; and, with colonies sent out by herself, they formed the so called Libyo-Phoenician population, open to the attack of all, and incapable of defence. Thus the country around Carthage was weak, and the moment a foreign enemy landed in Africa the war was merely a siege of its chief city.

The power of Carthage lay in her commerce. Through her hands passed the gold and pearls of the Orient; the famous Tyrian purple; ivory, slaves, and incense of Arabia; the silver of Spain; the bronze of Cyprus; and the iron of Elba.

But the harsh and gloomy character of the people, their cruel religion, which sanctioned human sacrifice, their disregard of the rights of others, their well known treachery, all shut them off from the higher civilization of Rome and Greece.

The government of Carthage was an **Aristocracy**. A council composed of a few of high birth, and another composed of the very wealthy, managed the state. Only in times of extraordinary danger were the people summoned and consulted.

Rome had made two treaties with Carthage; one immediately after the establishment of the Republic, in 500, the other about 340. By these treaties commerce was allowed between Rome and its dependencies and Carthage and her possessions in Sicily, Sardinia, and Corsica. But the Romans were not to trade in Spain, or sail beyond the Bay of Carthage.

In leaving Sicily, Pyrrhus had exclaimed, "What a fine battlefield for Rome and Carthage!" If Carthage were mistress of this island, Rome would be shut up in her peninsula; Rome were in possession of it, the commerce of Cartage would be intercepted, and a good breeze of one night would carry the Roman fleets to her walls.

At this time the island was shared by three powers,—**Hiero** of Syracuse, the **Carthaginians**, and the **Mamertimes**, a band of brigands who came from Campania. The latter, making Messána their headquarters, had been pillaging all of the island that they could reach. Being shut up in Messána by Hiero, they asked aid of Rome on the ground that they were from Campania. Although Rome was in alliance with Hiero, and had but recently executed 300 mercenaries for doing in Rhegium what the Mamertines had done in Sicily, she determined to aid them, for Sicily was a rich and tempting prey.

Meanwhile, however, through the intervention of the Carthaginians, a truce had been formed between Hiero and the brigands, and the siege of Messána was raised. The city itself was occupied by a fleet and garrison of Carthaginians under **Hanno**. The Romans, though the Mamertines no longer needed their aid, landed at Messána and dislodged the Carthaginians.

Thus opened the **First Punic**[1] **War**. The Romans at once formed a double alliance with Syracuse and Messána, thus gaining control of the eastern coast of Sicily and getting their first foothold outside of Italy.

The most important inland city of Sicily was **Agrigentum**. Here the Carthaginians the next year (262) concentrated their forces under **Hannibal**, son of Gisco. The Romans besieged the city, but were themselves cut off from supplies by Hanno, who landed at **Heracléa** in their rear. Both besieged and besiegers suffered much. At last a bat-

---

1 The word "Punic" is derived from *Phoenici*. The Carthaginians were said to have come originally from Phoenicia, on the eastern coast of the Mediterranean. Their first ruler was Dido. The Latin student is of course familiar with Virgil's story of Dido and Aenéas.

tle was fought (262), in which the Romans were victorious, owing to their superior infantry. Agrigentum fell, and only a few strongholds on the coast were left to the Carthaginians.

The Romans now began to feel the need of a fleet. That of Carthage ruled the sea without a rival: it not only controlled many of the seaports of Sicily, but also threatened Italy itself. With their usual energy, the Romans began the work. [2] A wrecked Carthaginian vessel was taken as a model, and by the spring of 260 a navy of 120 sail was ready for sea.

The ships were made the more formidable by a heavy iron beak, for the purpose of running down and sinking the enemy's vessels; a kind of hanging stage was also placed on the prow of the ship, which could be lowered in front or on either side. It was furnished on both sides with parapets, and had space for two men in front. On coming to close quarters with the enemy, this stage was quickly lowered and fastened to the opposing ship by means of grappling irons; thus the Roman marines were enabled to board with ease their opponents' ship, and fight as if on land.

Four naval battles now followed: 1st, near **Lipara** (260); 2nd, off **Mylae** (260); 3rd, off **Tyndaris** (257); 4th, off **Ecnomus** (256).

In the first of these only seventeen ships of the Romans were engaged under the Consul **Gnaeus Cornelius Scipio**. The fleet with its commander was captured.

In the second engagement, off Mylae, all the Roman fleet under **Gaius Duilius** took part. The Carthaginians were led by Hannibal, son of Gisco. The newly invented stages or boarding-bridges of the Romans were found to be very effective. The enemy could not approach near without these bridges descending with their grappling irons and holding them fast to the Romans. The Carthaginians were defeated, with the loss of nearly half their fleet.

A bronze column, ornamented with the beaks of the captured vessels, was erected at Rome in honour of this victory of Duilius. The pedestal of it is still standing, and on it are inscribed some of the oldest inscriptions in the Latin language.

The third engagement, off Tyndaris, resulted in a drawn battle.

In the fourth engagement, off Ecnomus, the Carthaginians had 350 sail. Thirty Carthaginian and twenty-four Roman vessels were sunk, and sixty-four of the former captured. The Punic fleet withdrew

---

2. In 259, three years previous to the battle of Ecnomus, the Romans under Lucius Scipio captured Blesia, a seaport of Corsica, and established there a naval station.

to the coast of Africa, and prepared in the Bay of Carthage for another battle. But the Romans sailed to the eastern side of the peninsula which helps to form the bay, and there landed without opposition.

Marcus Atilius Regulus was put in command of the Roman forces in Africa. For a time he was very successful, and the Carthaginians became disheartened. Many of the towns near Carthage surrendered, and the capital itself was in danger. Peace was asked, but the terms offered were too humiliating to be accepted.

Regulus, who began to despise his opponents, remained inactive at Tunis, near Carthage, neglecting even to secure a line of retreat to his fortified camp at Clupea. The next spring (255) he was surprised, his army cut to pieces, and he himself taken prisoner. He subsequently died a captive at Carthage.

The Romans, learning of this defeat, sent a fleet of 350 sail to relieve their comrades who were shut up in Clupea. While on its way, it gained a victory over the Carthaginian fleet off the Herméan promontory, sinking 114 of the enemy's ships. It arrived at Clupea in time to save its friends.

The war in Africa was now abandoned. The fleet, setting sail for home, was partly destroyed in a storm, only eighty ships reaching port.

Hostilities continued for six years without any great results. Panormus was taken in 254; the coast of Africa ravaged in 253; Thermae and the island of Lipara were taken in 252, and Eryx in 249.

Drepana and **Lilybaeum** were now the only places in Sicily held by Carthage. A regular siege of Lilybaeum was decided upon, and the city was blockaded by land and sea; but the besieging party suffered as much as the besieged, its supplies were frequently cut off by the cavalry of the Carthaginians, and its ranks began to be thinned by disease.

The Consul, Publius Claudius, who had charge of the siege, determined to surprise the Carthaginian fleet, which was stationed at Drepana (249). He was unsuccessful, and lost three fourths of his vessels. Another fleet of 120 sail sent to aid him was wrecked in a violent storm.

The Romans were now in perplexity. The war had lasted fifteen years. Four fleets had been lost, and one sixth of the fighting population. They had failed in Africa, and the two strongest places in Sicily were still in the enemy's hands. For six years more the war dragged on (249-243).

A new Carthaginian commander, **Hamilcar Barca** (Lightning), meanwhile took the field in Sicily. He was a man of great activity and military talent, and the Romans at first were no match for him. He seemed in a fair way to regain all Sicily. The apathy of the Senate was so great, that at last some private citizens built and manned at their own expense a fleet of 200 sail.

Gaius Lutatius Catulus, the Consul in command, surprised the enemy and occupied the harbours of Drepana and Lilybaeum in 242. A Carthaginian fleet which, came to the rescue was met and destroyed off the **Aegátes Insulae** in 241. Hamilcar was left in Sicily without support and supplies. He saw that peace must be made.

Sicily was surrendered. Carthage agreed to pay the cost of the war,—about $3,000,000,—one third down, and the remainder in ten annual payments. Thus ended the First Punic War.

CHAPTER 13

Rome and Carthage Between the First and Second Punic Wars (241-218)

Twenty-three years elapsed between the First and Second Punic Wars. The Carthaginians were engaged during the first part of this time in crushing a mutiny of their mercenary troops.

Rome, taking advantage of the position in which her rival was placed, seized upon **Sardinia** and **Corsica**, and, when Carthage objected, threatened to renew the war, and obliged her to pay more than one million dollars as a fine (237).

The acquisition of Sicily, Sardinia, and Corsica introduced into the government of Rome a new system; *viz.* the **Provincial System.**

Heretofore the two chief magistrates of Rome, the Consuls, had exercised their functions over all the Roman possessions. Now Sicily was made what the Romans called a *provincia*, or **Province.** Sardinia and Corsica formed another province (235).

Over each province was placed a Roman governor, called **Proconsul.** For this purpose two new *Praetors* were now elected, making four in all. The power of the governor was absolute; he was commander in chief, chief magistrate, and supreme judge.

The finances of the provinces were intrusted to one or more **Quaestors.** All the inhabitants paid as taxes into the Roman treasury one tenth of their produce, and five *per cent* of the value of their imports and exports. They were not obliged to furnish troops, as were the dependants of Rome in Italy.

The provincial government was a fruitful source of corruption. As the morals of the Romans degenerated, the provinces were plundered without mercy to enrich the coffers of the avaricious governors.

The Adriatic Sea at this time was overrun by Illyrican pirates, who did much damage. Satisfaction was demanded by Rome of Illyricum, but to no purpose. As a last resort, war was declared, and the sea was cleared of the pirates in 229.

"The results of this Illyrican war did not end here, for it was the means of establishing, for the first time, direct political relations between Rome and the states of Greece, to many of which the suppression of piracy was of as much importance as to Rome herself. Alliances were concluded with **Corcýra**, **Epidamnus**, and **Apollonia**; and embassies explaining the reasons which had brought Roman troops into Greece were sent to the Aetolians and Achaeans, to Athens and Corinth. The admission of the Romans to the Isthmian Games in 228 formally acknowledged them as the allies of the Greek states."

The Romans now began to look with hungry eyes upon **Gallia Cisalpína**. The appetite for conquest was well whetted. There had been peace with the Gauls since the battle of Lake Vadimónis in 283. The *ager publicus*, taken from the Gauls then, was still mostly unoccupied. In 232 the Tribune Gaius Flaminius[1] carried an agrarian law, to the effect that this land be given to the veterans and the poorer classes. The law was executed, and colonies planted. To the Gauls this seemed but the first step to the occupation of the whole of their country. They all rose in arms except the Cenománi.

This contest continued for ten years, and in 225 Etruria was invaded by an army of 70,000 men. The plans of the invaders, however, miscarried, and they were hemmed in between two Roman armies near **Telamon** in 222, and annihilated. The Gallic king was slain at the hands of the Consul **Marcus Claudius Marcellus**.

Rome was now mistress of the whole peninsula of Italy, excepting some tribes in Liguria, who resisted a short time longer.

Three *military* (Latin) colonies were founded to hold the Gauls in check; **Placentia** and **Cremóna** in the territory of the Insubres, and **Mutina** in that of the Boii. The *Via Flaminia*, the great northern road, was extended from **Spoletium** to **Ariminum**.[2]

Meanwhile Carthage was not idle. After subduing the revolt of

---

1. Gaius Flaminius, by his agrarian laws gained the bitter hatred of the nobility. He was the first Governor of Sicily, and there showed himself to be a man of integrity and honesty, a great contrast to many who succeeded him.
2. During this period the *Comitia Centuriáta* was reorganized on the (35) instead of money.

the mercenaries in 237, she formed the project of obtaining **Spain** as compensation for the loss of Sicily, Sardinia, and Corsica. Hamilcar Barca, by energetic measures, established (236-228) a firm foothold in Southern and South-eastern Spain.

At his death, his son-in-law, Hasdrubal, continued his work. Many towns were founded, trade prospered, and agriculture flourished. The discovery of rich silver mines near Carthágo Nova was a means of enriching the treasury. After the assassination of Hasdrubal, in 220, the ablest leader was **Hannibal**, son of Hamilcar. Although a young man of but twenty-eight, he had had a life of varied experience. As a boy he had shown great courage and ability in camp under his father. He was a fine athlete, well educated in the duties of a soldier, and could endure long privation of sleep and food. For the last few years he had been in command of the cavalry, and had distinguished himself for personal bravery, as well as by his talents as a leader.

Hannibal resolved to begin the inevitable struggle with Rome at once. He therefore laid siege to **Saguntum**, a Spanish town allied to Rome. In eight months the place was compelled to capitulate (219).

When Rome demanded satisfaction of Carthage for this insult, and declared herself ready for war, the Carthaginians accepted the challenge, and the **Second Punic War** began in 218.

CHAPTER 14

The Second Punic War—From the Passage of the Pyrenees to the Battle of Cannae (218-216)

In the spring of 218 Hannibal started from Carthágo Nova to invade Italy. His army consisted of 90,000 infantry, 12,000 cavalry, and 37 elephants. His march to the Pyrenees occupied two months, owing to the opposition of the Spanish allies of Rome. Hannibal now sent back a part of his troops, retaining 50,000 infantry and 9,000 cavalry, all veterans. With these he crossed the mountains, and marched along the coast by Narbo (Narbonne) and Nemansus (Nimes), through the Celtic territory, with little opposition. The last of July found him on the banks of the Rhone, opposite Avenio (Avignon). The Romans were astonished at the rapidity of his movements.

The Consuls of the year were **Scipio** and **Sempronius**. The former had been in Northern Italy, leisurely collecting forces to attack Hannibal in Spain; the latter was in Sicily, making preparations to invade Africa. Scipio set sail for Spain, touching at Massilia near the end of June. Learning there for the first time that Hannibal had already left Spain, he hoped to intercept him on the Rhone. The Celtic tribes of the neighbourhood were won over to his side. Troops collected from these were stationed along the river, but Scipio's main army remained at Massilia.

It was Hannibal's policy to cross the river before Scipio arrived with his troops. He obtained all the boats possible, and constructed numerous rafts to transport his main body of troops. A detachment of soldiers was sent up the river with orders to cross at the first available place, and, returning on the opposite bank, to surprise the Celtic forces in the rear. The plan succeeded. The Celts fled in confusion, and the road to the Alps was opened. Thus Scipio was outgeneralled in the very beginning.

His course now should have been to return to Northern Italy with all his forces, and take every means to check Hannibal there. Instead, he sent most of his troops to Spain under his brother Gnaeus Scipio, and himself, with but a few men, set sail for Pisae.

Meanwhile Hannibal hurried up the valley of the Rhone, across the Isara, through the fertile country of the Allobroges, arriving, in sixteen days from Avenio, at the pass of the first Alpine range (Mont du Chat). Crossing this with some difficulty, owing to the nature of the country and the resistance of the Celts, he hastened on through the country of the Centrónes, along the north bank of the Isara. As he was leaving this river and approaching the pass of the Little St. Bernard, he was again attacked by the Celts, and obliged to make the ascent amidst continual and bloody encounters. After toiling a day and a night, however, the army reached the summit of the pass. Here, on a tableland, his troops were allowed a brief rest.

The hardships of the descent were fully as great, and the fertile valley of the Po was a welcome sight to the half-famished and exhausted soldiers. Here they encamped, in September, and recruited their wearied energies.

This famous march of Hannibal from the Rhone lasted thirty-three days, and cost him 20,000 infantry and 3,000 cavalry.

The Romans were still unprepared to meet Hannibal. One army was in Spain under Gnaeus Scipio; the other in Sicily, on its way to Africa, under the Consul Sempronius. The only troops immediately available were a few soldiers that had been left in the valley of the Po to restrain the Gauls, who had recently shown signs of defection.

Publius Cornelius Scipio, upon his return from Massilia, took command of these. He met Hannibal first in October, 218, near the River **Ticínus**, a tributary of the Po. A cavalry skirmish followed, in which he was wounded and rescued by his son, a lad of seventeen, afterwards the famous **Africánus**. The Romans were discomfited, with considerable loss.

They then retreated, crossing the Po at Placentia, and destroying the bridge behind them. Hannibal forded the river farther up, and marched along its right bank until he reached its confluence with the **Trebia**, opposite Placentia. Here he encamped.

Meanwhile Sempronius, who had been recalled from Sicily, relieved the disabled Scipio.

One raw morning in December, 218, the vanguard of the Carthaginians was ordered to cross the Trebia, and, as soon any resistance was met, to retreat. The other troops of Hannibal were drawn up ready to give the enemy a hot reception, if, as he expected, they should pursue his retreating vanguard. Sempronius was caught in the trap, and all his army, except one division of 10,000, was cut to pieces. The survivors took refuge in Placentia and Cremóna, where they spent the winter. Sempronius himself escaped to Rome.

The result of **Trebia** was the insurrection of all the Celtic tribes in the valley of the Po, who increased Hannibal's army by 60,000 infantry and 4,000 cavalry. While the Carthaginian was wintering near Placentia, the Romans stationed troops to guard the two highways leading north from Rome and ending at Arretium and Ariminum. The Consuls for this year were **Gaius Flaminius** and **Gnaeus Servilius**. The former occupied Arretium, the latter Ariminum. Here they were joined by the troops that had wintered at Placentia.

In the spring, Hannibal, instead of attempting to pursue his march by either of the highways which were fortified, outflanked the Romans by turning aside into Etruria. His route led through a marshy and unhealthy country, and many soldiers perished. Hannibal himself lost an eye from ophthalmia. When he had arrived at Faesulae a report of his course first reached Flaminius, who at once broke camp and endeavoured to intercept his enemy. Hannibal, however, had the start, and was now near **Lake Trasiménus**.

Here was a pass with a high hill on one side and the lake on the other. Hannibal, with the flower of his infantry, occupied the hill. His light-armed troops and horsemen were drawn up in concealment on either side.

The Roman column advanced (May, 217), without hesitation, to the unoccupied pass, the thick morning mist completely concealing the position of the enemy. As the Roman vanguard approached the hill, Hannibal gave the signal for attack. The cavalry closed up the entrance to the pass, and at the same time the mist rolled away, revealing the Carthaginian arms on the right and left. It was not a battle, but a mere rout. The main body of the Romans was cut to pieces, with scarcely any resistance, and the Consul himself was killed. Fifteen thousand Romans fell, and as many more were captured. The loss of the Carthaginians was but 1,500, and was confined mostly to the Gallic allies. All Etruria was lost, and Hannibal could march without hindrance upon Rome, whose citizens, expecting the enemy daily, tore down the bridges over the Tiber and prepared for a siege. **Quintus Fabius Maximus** was appointed Dictator.

Hannibal, however, did not march upon Rome, but turned through Umbria, devastating the country as he went. Crossing the Apennines, he halted on the shores of the Adriatic, in Picénum. After giving his army a rest, he proceeded along the coast into Southern Italy.

The Romans, seeing that the city was not in immediate danger, raised another army, and placed the Dictator in command. Fabius was a man of determination and firmness, well advanced in years. He determined to avoid a pitched battle, but to dog the steps of the enemy, harassing him and cutting off his supplies as far as possible.

Meanwhile Hannibal again crossed the mountains into the heart of Italy to Beneventum, and from there to **Capua**, the largest Italian city dependent upon Rome. The Dictator followed, condemning his soldiers to the melancholy task of looking on in inaction, while the enemy's cavalry plundered their faithful allies. Finally, Fabius obtained what he considered a favourable opportunity for an attack. Hannibal, disappointed in his expectations that Capua would be friendly to him, and not being prepared to lay siege to the town, had withdrawn towards the Adriatic. Fabius intercepted him near **Casilínum**, in Campania, on the left bank of the Volturnus. The heights that commanded the right bank of the river were occupied by his main army; and the road itself, which led across the river, was guarded by a strong division of men.

Hannibal, however, ordered his light-armed troops to ascend the heights over the road during the night, driving before them oxen with burning fagots tied to their horns, giving the appearance of an army marching by torchlight. The plan was successful. The Romans abandoned the road and marched for the heights, along which they supposed the enemy were going. Hannibal, with a clear road before him, continued his march with the bulk of his army. The next morning he recalled his light-armed troops, which had been sent on to the hills with the oxen. Their engagement with the Romans had resulted in a severe loss to Fabius.

Hannibal then proceeded, without opposition, in a north-easterly direction, by a very circuitous route. He arrived in Luceria, with much booty and a full money-chest, at harvest time. Near here he encamped in a plain rich in grain and grass for the support of his army.

At Rome the policy of Fabius was severely criticised. His apparent inaction was displeasing to a large party, and he was called **Cunctá-tor** (the Delayer). At length the assembly voted that his command be shared by one of his lieutenants, Marcus Minucius. The army was divided into two corps; one under Marcus, who intended to attack Hannibal at the first opportunity; the other under Fabius, who still adhered to his former tactics. Marcus made an attack, but paid dearly for his rashness, and his whole corps would have been annihilated had not Fabius come to his assistance and covered his retreat. Hannibal passed the winter of 217-216 unmolested.

The season was spent by the Romans in active preparations for the spring campaign. An army of 80,000 infantry and 6,000 cavalry was raised and put under the command of the Consuls, **Lucius Æmilius Paullus** and **Gaius Terentius Varro**. It was decided to test Hannibal's strength once more in open battle. His army was only half as strong as the Roman in infantry, but was much superior in cavalry.

In the early summer of 216 the Consuls concentrated their forces at **Cannae**, a hamlet near the mouth of the Aufidus. Early one morning in June the Romans massed their troops on the left bank of the river, with their cavalry on either wing, the right under Paullus, and the left under Varro. The Proconsul Servilius commanded the centre.

The Carthaginians were drawn up in the form of a crescent, flanked by cavalry. Both armies advanced to the attack at the same time. The onset was terrible; but though the Romans fought with a courage increased by the thought that their homes, wives, and children were at stake, they were overwhelmed on all sides. Seventy thousand fell on the field, among whom were Paullus, Servilius, many officers, and eighty men of senatorial rank. This was the most crushing defeat ever experienced by the Romans. All Southern Italy, except the Latin colonies and the Greek cities on the coast, went over to Hannibal

CHAPTER 15

The Second Punic War—From Cannae to the Battle of Zama (216-202)

Rome was appalled; but though defeated, she was not subdued. All the Latin allies were summoned for aid in the common peril. Boys and old men alike took up arms; even the slaves were promised freedom if they would join the ranks.

Hannibal marched from Cannae into Campania. He induced Capua, the second city of Italy, to side with him. But his expectations that other cities would follow her example were not fulfilled. He went into winter quarters here (215-214). The Capuans, notorious for their luxurious and effeminate habits, are said to have injured his soldiers. But Hannibal's superiority as a general is unquestionable, and his want of success after this was due to insufficient aid from home, and to the fact that the resources of Rome were greater than those of Carthage. The Latin allies of Rome had remained true to their allegiance, and only one city of importance was under his control. It was an easy matter to conquer the enemy in open battle, but to support his own army was more difficult, for all Italy had been devastated. On the other hand, the Romans were well supplied with food from their possessions in Sicily.

Hannibal saw, therefore, that more active measures than those already employed were necessary. He sent to Carthage an appeal for aid. He formed an alliance with **Philip V**. of Macedonia, and earnestly urged **Hasdrubal Barca**, his lieutenant in Spain, to come to his assistance. He hoped, with this army from the north, with supplies and reinforcements from Carthage, and with such troops as he might obtain from Macedonia, to concentrate a large force at Rome and compel her into submission.

The Romans, realizing the position of Hannibal, kept what forces they could spare in Spain, under the two Scipio brothers, Publius and Gnaeus. With these they hoped to stop reinforcements from reaching the enemy from that quarter. At the same time their army in Northern Greece effectually engaged the attention of Philip. Thus two years (214-212) passed without any material change in the situation of affairs in Italy.

In 212, while the Carthaginians were in the extreme south of Italy, besieging Tarentum, the Romans made strenuous efforts to recover Campania, and especially Capua. Hannibal, learning the danger, marched rapidly north, and failing to break through the lines which enclosed the city, resolved to advance on Rome itself.

Silently and quickly he marched along the *Via Latina* through the heart of the territory of Rome, to within three miles of the city, and with his vanguard he even rode up to one of the city gates. But no ally joined him; no Roman force was recalled to face him; no proposals of peace reached his camp. Impressed by the unmoved confidence of the enemy, he withdrew as quickly as he came, and retreated to his headquarters in the South.

Capua fell in 211, and the seat of war, to the great relief of Rome, was removed to Lucania and Bruttium. The punishment inflicted upon Capua was severe. Seventy of her Senators were killed, three hundred of her chief citizens imprisoned, and the whole people sold as slaves. The city and its territory were declared to be Roman territory, and the place was afterwards repeopled by Roman occupants.

Such was the fate of this famous city. Founded in as early times as Rome itself, it became the most flourishing city of Magna Graecia, renowned for its luxury and refinement, and as the home of all the highest arts and culture.

AFFAIRS IN SICILY.

Hiero II., tyrant of Syracuse, died in 216. During his long reign of more than fifty years he had been the stanch friend and ally of Rome in her struggles with Carthage. Hieronymus, the grandson and successor of Hiero, thought fit to ally himself with Carthage. The young tyrant, who was arrogant and cruel, was assassinated after reigning a few months.

The Roman Governor of Sicily, **Marcellus**, troubled by the

Carthaginian faction in Syracuse, threatened the city with an attack unless the leaders of this faction were expelled. In return, they endeavoured to arouse the citizens of the neighbouring city of Leontíni against Rome and the Roman party in Syracuse. Marcellus at once attacked and stormed Leontíni. The Syracusans then closed their city gates against him. A siege of two years (214-212) followed, famous for the various devices adopted by the noted mathematician **Archimédes**[1] to defeat the movements of the Romans. The city was finally betrayed by a Spanish officer, and given up to plunder. The art treasures in which it was so rich were conveyed by Marcellus to Rome. From this time (212) the city became a part of the province of Sicily and the headquarters of the Roman Governor.

THE CAMPAIGNS IN SPAIN.

Publius Cornelius Scipio, with his brother, **Gnaeus Cornelius Scipio Calvus**, were winning victories over the Carthaginians under **Hanno** and **Hasdrubal**. The greatest of these was fought in 215 at Ibera, the location of which is uncertain. Spain was gradually being gained over to Rome, when the Carthaginians, making desperate efforts, sent large reinforcements there (212). The armies of the Scipios were separated, surprised, and overwhelmed. Both their leaders were slain, and Spain was lost to Rome.

Unless checked, the Carthaginians would now cross the Alps, enter Italy, and, joining forces with Hannibal, place Rome in great danger. **Publius Cornelius Scipio**, son of one of the slain generals, then but twenty-four years of age, offered to go to Spain and. take command. He had previously made himself very popular as Aedile, and was unanimously elected to the command. On his arrival in Spain in 210, he found the whole country west of the Ebro under the enemy's control.

Fortunately for the Romans, the three Carthaginian generals, **Hasdrubal** and **Mago**, brothers of Hannibal, and **Hasdrubal**, son of Gisco, did not act in harmony. Thus Scipio was enabled, in the follow-

---

1. Archimédes was a great investigator in the science of mathematics. He discovered the ratio of a sphere to its circumscribed cylinder. One of his famous sayings was, "*Give me where to stand, and I will move the world.*" He exerted his ingenuity in the invention of powerful machines for the defence of Syracuse. Eight of his works on mathematics are in existence. He was killed at the close of the siege by a Roman soldier, who would have spared his life had he not been too intent on a mathematical problem to comply with the summons to surrender. On his tombstone, it is said, was engraved a cylinder enclosing a sphere.

ing spring (209), to capture Carthágo Nova, the headquarters of the enemy. A good harbour was gained, and eighteen ships of war, sixty-three transports, $600,000, and 10,000 captives fell into the hands of the Romans.

Shortly after, Scipio fought Hasdrubal, the brother of Hannibal, at **Baeculae**, in the upper valley of the Baetis (Guadalquivir); but the battle was not decisive, for Hasdrubal was soon seen crossing the Pyrenees, with a considerable force, on his way to Italy. He spent the winter (209-208) in Gaul.

The two Carthaginian generals now in Spain, Mago, and Hasdrubal, the son of Gisco, retired, the latter to Lusitania, the former to the Baleares, to wait for reinforcements from home.

The next year another battle was fought near Baecula, resulting in the total defeat of the Carthaginians, who retreated to Gadus, in the south-western part of Spain.

The country being now (206) under Roman influence, Scipio crossed the straits to Africa, and visited the Numidian princes, **Syphax** and **Masinissa**, whom he hoped to stir up against Carthage. On his return, after quelling a mutiny of the soldiers, who were dissatisfied about their pay, he resigned his command, and started for Rome, where he intended to become a candidate for the consulship.

OPERATIONS IN ITALY.

The news of the approach of Hasdrubal caused intense anxiety at Rome. Every nerve was strained to prevent the union of the two brothers. The Consuls for this year (207) were **Gaius Claudìus Nero**, a patrician, and **Marcus Livius**, a plebeian. To the former was intrusted the task of keeping Hannibal in check in Bruttium, while the duty of intercepting Hasdrubal was given to the latter.

The Carthaginian had already reached the neighbourhood of the River Metaurus, a small stream south of the Rubicon. From here he sent messengers to inform his brother of his approach and proposed line of march. These messengers were captured by Nero, and the contents of their despatches learned. He at once pushed north with his forces, joined Livius, met Hasdrubal on the **Metaurus** early in 207, and defeated his army with great slaughter. Among the slain was Hasdrubal himself. Nero returned south without delay, and the first intimation that Hannibal had of this battle was the sight of his brother's head thrown into the camp by the victorious foe.

The war in Italy was now virtually ended, for, although during four years more Hannibal stood at bay in a corner of Bruttium, he was powerless to prevent the restoration of Roman authority throughout Italy. Nothing now remained to Carthage outside of Africa, except the ground on which was making his last stand.

INVASION OF AFRICA.

Scipio, on his return from Spain, urged an immediate invasion of Africa. He was elected Consul in 205, receiving Sicily as his province, with permission to cross into Africa if it seemed to him wise. He was so popular that voluntary contributions of men, money, and supplies poured in from all sides. The old-fashioned aristocracy, however, did not like him, as his taste for splendid living and Greek culture was particularly offensive to them; and a party in the Senate would have recalled him, had not the popular enthusiasm in his favour been too strong to be resisted.

In 204 he sailed from Lilybaeum, and landed near Utica. He was welcomed by Masinissa, whose friendship he had gained in his previous visit to Africa from Spain. Syphax, however, sided with Carthage; but in 203 Scipio twice defeated him and the Carthaginian forces.

Negotiations for peace followed, but the war party in Carthage prevailed. Hannibal was recalled. He returned to fight his last battle with Rome, October 19, 202, at **Zama**, a short distance west of Carthage. The issue was decided by the valour of the Roman legions, who loved their commander and trusted his skill. Hannibal met his first and only defeat, and Scipio won his title of **Africánus**. The battle was a hard one. After all the newly enrolled troops of Hannibal had been killed or put to flight, his veterans, who had remained by him in Italy, although surrounded on all sides by forces far outnumbering their own, fought on, and were killed one by one around their beloved chief. The army was fairly annihilated. Hannibal, with only a handful, managed to escape to Hadrumétum.

The Battle of Zama decided the fate of the West The power of Carthage was broken, and her supremacy passed to Rome. She was allowed to retain her own territory intact, but all her warships, except ten, were given up, and her prisoners restored; an annual tax of about $200,000, for fifty years, was to be paid into the Roman treasury, and she could carry on no war without the consent of Rome. Masinissa was rewarded by an increase in territory, and was enrolled among the "allies and friends of the Roman people."

Rome was now safe from any attack. She had become a great

Mediterranean power. Spain was divided into two provinces, and the north of Africa was under her protection.

Such was the result of the seventeen years' struggle. Scipio was welcomed home, and surnamed **Africánus**. He enjoyed a triumph never before equalled. His statue was placed, in triumphal robes and crowned with laurels, in the Capitol. Many honours were thrust upon him, which he had the sense to refuse. He lived quietly for some years, taking no part in politics.

CHAPTER 16

Rome in the East

Rome was now in a position to add new nations to her list of subjects. The kingdoms of the East which formerly composed a part of the vast empire of Alexander the Great, and which finally went to swell the limits of Roman authority, were Egypt, Syria, Macedonia, and Greece proper.

Egypt was governed by the Ptolemies, and included at this time the valley of the Nile, Palestine, Phoenicia, the Island of Cyprus, and a number of towns in Thrace.

Syria, extending from the Mediterranean to the Indus, was composed of various nations which enjoyed a semi-independence. Under incompetent rulers, she saw portion after portion of her dominions fall from her. Thus arose Pergamus, Pontus, Cappadocia, and Phrygia.

Macedonia was ruled by Philip V., and included also a large portion of Northern Greece.

Greece proper was divided between the **Achaean** and **Aetolian Leagues**, the former including the most of the Peloponnésus, the latter the greater part of Central Greece.

Ever since the repulse of Pyrrhus, Rome had been slowly drifting into closer contact with the East. She formed an alliance with Egypt in 273. From this country had come in part her Supply of corn during the Second Punic War. In 205, Ptolemy V. became king, and, through fear of the Macedonian and Syrian kings, sought the protection of Rome.

The punishment of the Illyrican pirates in 228 brought Rome into closer relations with Greece. These connections had been sufficient to open the Eastern ports to her trade, but her struggle with Carthage had left her no time or strength to interfere actively in Eastern politics, until she was forced to take action by the alliance of Philip V. of Macedonia and Hannibal, and by the former's threatened invasion of Italy in 214. A small force was sent into Greece, which was soon largely increased by the dissatisfied subjects of Philip.

The only object of Rome in the **First Macedonian War** (214-205) was to prevent Philip from lending aid to Hannibal; and in this she was partially successful. None of the Macedonian troops entered Italy, but four thousand of them were at Zama.

The military operations of this war were of slight importance. Marcus Valerius Laevínus was sent to the Adriatic, and pushed the king so hard that he was obliged to burn the fleet in which he intended to sail for Italy. Philip was at this time at war with Aetolia. Laevínus assisted the Aetolians, and the king was too fully occupied at home to think of operations farther away. But in 205, the Romans, wishing to concentrate their energies upon the invasion of Africa, made peace.

Some of Philip's soldiers had been captured at Zama. He demanded their return. The answer was, that, if he wished war again, he could have it.

There were several other reasons which led to the **Second Macedonian War** (200-197). Philip had agreed with **Antiochus III.**, king of Syria, to attempt with him the division of Egypt, since it seemed probable that the young king, Epiphanes (Ptolemy V.), who was only four years old, would not be able to make an effectual resistance. The ministers of Egypt sought the protection of Rome. On their journey, the Roman envoys sent to assume the office of protectorship remonstrated with Philip.

In Asia Minor Philip had conducted himself with such barbarity that the people rose against him; and from a similar cause Greece was driven to seek alliances which would protect her against him.

Rome was unwilling to undertake a new war, but the people were induced to vote for one, on the representation that the only means of preventing an invasion of Italy was to carry the war abroad.

This year (200) the Consul, Publius Sulpicius Galba, was sent with a considerable force across the Adriatic. His campaign, and that of the Consul Villius during the next year, were productive of no decisive results, but in 198 the Consul **Titus Quinctius Flaminínus**, a man of different calibre, conducted the war with vigour. He defeated Philip on the Aóus, drove him back to the pass of Tempe, and the next year utterly defeated him at Cynoscephalae .

The king had drawn up his forces in two divisions. With the first he broke through the line of the legions, which, however, closed in around him with but little loss. The other division was attacked by the Romans, while it was forming, and thoroughly discomfited. The victory of the Romans was decisive.

About the same time the Achaeans captured Corinth from Philip, and the Rhodians defeated his troops in Caria. Further resistance was impossible. Philip was left in possession of Macedonia alone; he was deprived of all his dependencies in Greece, Thrace, and Asia Minor, and was forbidden, as Carthage had been, to wage war without Rome's consent.

The next year (196), at the Isthmian Games, the "freedom of Greece" was proclaimed to the enthusiastic crowds, and two years later Flamanínus withdrew his troops from the so called "three fetters of Greece,"—Chalcis, Demetrias, and Corinth,—and, urging the Greeks to show themselves worthy of the gift of the Roman people, he returned home to enjoy a well earned triumph.

The chief result of the second Macedonian war was, therefore, the firm establishment of a **Roman Protectorate over Greece and Egypt**. The wedge had been entered and the interference of Rome in Eastern affairs was assured.

CHAPTER 17

The Syrian War

Antiochus III. of Syria, who had proposed to share Egypt with Philip, had been engaged for some time in a campaign in the East, and did not hear of his ally's danger until too late to aid him. However, he claimed for himself portions of Asia Minor and Thrace, which Philip had previously held, and which Rome now declared free and independent. He crossed the Hellespont into Thrace in 196, but did not dare to enter Greece, although earnestly urged to do so by the Aetolians, until after Flamininus had withdrawn all his troops (192).

Antiochus was no general. Himself irresolute and fond of pleasure, the power behind his throne was Hannibal. This great soldier, after his defeat at Zama, did not relinquish the aim of his life. He became the chief magistrate of his native city, and in a short time cleared the moral atmosphere, which was charged with corruption and depravity. Under him Carthage might have risen again. But his intrigues with Antiochus, with whom he wished to make an alliance, gave Rome an opportunity to interfere. His surrender was demanded. He fled, and, after wandering from coast to coast, became the trusted adviser of the Syrian king.

Had Antiochus been energetic after his arrival in Greece, he could have accomplished something before the Roman troops came. But he disregarded the warnings of Hannibal, and spent valuable time in minor matters. The Romans arrived in 191, and under Glabrio at Thermopylae drove back the intruder, who hastily retired to Asia Minor. The Aetolians were punished for their infidelity.

In 190, **Lucius Cornelius Scipio** was elected Consul, and put in command of the army in the East, with the understanding that he should be accompanied by his brother Africánus, and have the benefit of his military skill and experience. Under his command, the Romans crossed the Hellespont and sought Antiochus in his own kingdom.

Hannibal could do nothing with the poorly disciplined troops of the king. They were met by the invading forces at **Magnesia**, in Lydia, in 190, and 80,000 Asiatics were put to rout by 30,000 Romans, 50,000 being slain. The loss of the victors was slight.

On that day the fate of Asia was sealed. Antiochus relinquished all pretensions to any territory west of the River Halys and the Taurus mountains. His chariots, elephants, fleet, and treasures were all surrendered.

Scipio returned home to enjoy a triumph, and added **Asiaticus** to his name, as his brother had taken that of Africánus in commemoration of his victory.

Gneius Manlius Vulso succeeded Scipio in the East. He made a campaign against the Gauls, who had settled in Galatia about a century before, and had become wealthy by means of constant plunderings. The excuse for the campaign was, that they had served in the Syrian army; the reason was, their wealth, and the ambition of the Consul for glory.

The Galatians were easily overcome, their wealth seized, and they themselves became assimilated to their neighbours. This war is noticeable chiefly for the reason that Manlius undertook it *without the authority of the Senate*, the first instance of its kind, and a precedent which was too frequently followed in later times. On his return to Rome he was allowed a triumph, which stamped his act as legal.

These wars in the East brought to Rome immense riches, which laid the foundation of its Oriental extravagance and luxury, and finally undermined the strength of the state. From Greece were introduced learning and refinement, from Asia immorality and effeminacy. The vigour and tone of Roman society are nowhere more forcibly shown than in the length of time it took for its subjugation by these ruinous exotics.

Meanwhile, at Rome the political enemies of the Scipios were in the ascendency. Asiaticus was accused of misappropriating funds obtained during his campaign in the East. As he was about to produce his account-books before the Senate, his brother, Africánus, seized them, tore them to pieces, and threw the remnants on the floor. Asiaticus, however, was sentenced to pay a fine. When it was afterwards intimated that his brother too was implicated, he proudly reminded his enemies that their insinuations were ill timed, for it was the anniversary of Zama. This remark changed the tide of feeling, and no more charges were made.

Two years later (183), Africánus died in voluntary exile at Liternum, on the coast of Campania. He had lived little more than fifty years. His wife, Aemilia, was the daughter of Paullus, who fell at Cannae, and the sister of him who afterwards conquered Perseus of Macedonia. His daughter, **Cornelia**, afterwards became the mother of the famous **Gracchi**

Next to Caesar, Scipio was Rome's greatest general. During the campaign in the East, he met Hannibal at the court of Antiochus. In the conversation Hannibal is reported to have said that he considered Alexander the greatest general, Pyrrhus next, and, had he himself conquered Scipio, he would have placed himself before either.

Scipio lived to see Rome grow from an Italian power to be practically the mistress of the world. He was of marked intellectual culture, and as conversant with Greek as with his mother tongue. He possessed a charm which made him popular at a time when the culture and arts of Greece were not so courted at Rome as in later days.

Hannibal, after the defeat of Antiochus, was demanded by the Romans, but, escaping, took refuge in Crete, and subsequently with Prusias, King of Bithynia. His surrender was demanded, and troops were sent to arrest him. Seeing no way of escape, he opened the bead on his ring and swallowed the poison which it contained (183).

Thus died one of the greatest of commanders, without attaining the aim of his life. He had lived but fifty-four years, yet his life was so marked that people have ever since with wonder upon the tremendous magnitude of what he undertook, and came so near accomplishing.

This same year is also memorable for the death of "the last of the Greeks," **Philopoemen**. [1]

---

1 See *Ancient Greece.*

CHAPTER 18

Conquest of Macedonia and Greece (171-146)

Although Philip had aided the Romans in their campaign against Antiochus, he did not receive from them the expected reward in additions to his territory. Immediate resistance would be futile; but he laboured patiently and quietly to increase his resources, and to stir up among the neighbouring Greeks hostile feeling towards Rome. He placed his army on the best footing possible, and soon began to enlarge his boundaries. Complaints were made to Rome, and the king was compelled to give up his conquests, and confine himself to the limits of Macedonia. In 179 Philip died, and was succeeded by his son **Perseus**.

The new king was as able as his father, and more impatient of subjection. He made friends with the surrounding princes, formed a marriage connection with Antiochus IV. of Syria, and strove to arouse among the Greeks memories of their former greatness.

The Senate, hearing of his numerous intrigues, determined to check him. War was declared in 171; but the forces sent by Rome were at first led by incompetent men, and nothing was accomplished until **Lucius Aemilius Paullus** was made Consul, and took charge of the war in 168.

Paullus (229-160) was the son of the Consul of the same name who was killed at Cannae. His integrity was first shown when, as **Curule Aedile**,[1] in 192, he prosecuted persons who had made an illegal use of the public pastures. He was sent to Ulterior Spain in 191 as governor, where, after some reverses, he put down all insurrections.

---

1. See Chapter 45.

74

He was Consul in 182, and did good work in conquering a tribe of marauders in Liguria. For this he was allowed a triumph.

He was elected Consul a second time in 168, and sent against Perseus. The war was brought to a speedy end by the Battle of **Pydna**, on the Thermáic Gulf, June 22. The king fled to Samothrace with his treasures and family. He was shortly afterwards captured, but was treated with kindness by the Consul.

Paullus now travelled through Greece. Later, assisted by commissioners, he arranged the affairs of Macedonia. The country was divided into four small republics, independent of each other, but prohibited from intermarriage and commerce with one another.

On his return to Rome in 167, he enjoyed a triumph, which was graced by Perseus and his three children. He was Censor in 164, and died four years later.

Paullus had two sons by his first wife. The elder of these was adopted by Fabius Maximus Cunctátor, the younger by the son of Africánus the elder, his brother-in-law. He was of the "blue" blood of Rome, of perfect honesty, and very popular, a good general, but somewhat superstitious. A patron of learning and the fine arts, he gave his sons the best training under Greek masters. A strong proof of his popularity is the fact that his body was carried to its last resting place by volunteers from the various peoples he had conquered.

Perseus spent his last days in confinement near Rome, enduring, it is alleged, base and cruel treatment. He was the last king of Macedonia.

After the victory at Pydna, the sympathy shown in Greece for the conquered monarch made the Romans more watchful of her interests there. All suspected to be enemies were removed as hostages to Italy, and among these was the historian Polybius. He lived in Rome for more than twenty years, and became a great friend of the younger Africánus, whom he accompanied to the siege of Carthage.

Like Macedonia, Greece was separated into parts, independent of each other, with no rights of *connubium* or *commercium*. Utter demoralization soon ensued, which proved a sure preventive to all alliances liable to shake the authority of Rome.

Trouble again arose in Macedonia twenty years after Pydna, culminating in what is sometimes called the **Fourth Macedonian War** (149-146). Under the leadership of **Andriscus**, who claimed to be a son of Perseus, the people rebelled against the protection of Rome. They were twice defeated in 148 by the praetor **Quintus Caecilius**

Metellus, who gained the agnomen of **Macedonicus**. The country was made a Roman province, with a Roman magistrate at its head.

At this time the Achaeans were quarrelling with Sparta. Metellus warned them to desist, and when the Achaeans advanced against him, he easily defeated them near **Scarpheia**.

Metellus was a moderate reformer and a model man. He belonged to an illustrious plebeian *gens*, the Caecilian. Before his death in 115 three of his sons had been consuls, one censor, and the fourth was a candidate for consulship.

Metellus was succeeded in Greece by **Lucius Mummius**, a cruel and harsh leader. The remnant of the Achaean army had taken refuge in **Corinth**. The Senate directed Mummius to attack the city. Its capture in 146 was marked by special cruelties. The city was burned to the ground; beautiful pictures and costly statuary were ruthlessly destroyed. Gold in abundance was carried to Rome. The last vestige of Greek liberty vanished. The country became a Roman province under the name of **Achaia**.

Corinth, the "eye of all Greece," remained in ruins for a century, when it was rebuilt in 46 by Julius Caesar, who planted on its site a colony of veterans and freedmen.

CHAPTER 19

The Third Punic War, and Fall of Carthage

Fifty years had passed since Zama. It was a period of great commercial prosperity for Carthage, but her government was weakened by the quarrels of conflicting factions.

Masinissa, King of Numidia, an ally of the Romans, was a continual source of annoyance to Carthage. He made inroads upon her territory, and, as she was bound by her treaty not to war upon any allies of Rome, her only recourse was to complain to the Senate. In 157 an embassy was sent to inquire into the troubles. **Marcus Porcius Cato**, the chief of the embassy, was especially alarmed at the prosperity of the city, and from that time never ceased to urge its destruction. The embassy did not reach any decision, but allowed matters to go on as they might. Finally, when some sympathizers with Masinissa were banished from the city, he attacked and defeated the Carthaginians, compelled their army to pass under the yoke, and afterwards treacherously destroyed it (150). Carthage was compelled to give up some of her territory, and pay $5,000,000 indemnity.

After this victory, matters came to a crisis. The city must be disciplined for warring with an ally of Rome. Cato never failed to close any speech he might make in the Senate with the same cruel words, *Delenda est Carthago*, "Carthage must be destroyed."

The people of Carthage were called to account. Desponding and broken-hearted, they sent ambassadors to Rome. The answer given them was obscure. They were requested to make reparation to Rome, and at the same time they were assured that nothing should be undertaken against Carthage herself. But in 149 the Consuls crossed with a large army into Sicily, where the troops were organized, and Carthaginian ambassadors were expected.

When they appeared, the Consuls declared that the Senate did not wish to encroach upon the freedom of the people, but only desired some security; for this purpose it demanded that, within thirty days, three hundred children of the noblest families should be delivered into their hands as hostages. This demand was met. The Romans then coolly crossed over to Africa, and informed the Carthaginians that they were ready to treat with them on any question not previously settled.

When the ambassadors again appeared before the Consuls, they were told that Carthage must deliver over all her arms and artillery; for, they said, as Rome was able to protect her, there was no need of Carthage possessing arms. Hard as was this command, it was obeyed. They were then told that Carthage had indeed shown her goodwill, but that Rome had no control over the city so long as it was fortified. The preservation of peace, therefore, required that the people should quit the city, give up their navy, and build a new town without walls at a distance of ten miles from the sea. The indignation and fury which this demand excited were intense. The gates were instantly closed, and all the Romans and Italians who happened to be within the city were massacred.

The Romans, who expected to find a defenceless population, imagined that the storming of the place would be an easy matter. But despair had suggested to the Carthaginians means of defence in every direction. All assaults were repelled. Everybody was engaged day and night in the manufacture of arms. Nothing can be more heartrending than this last struggle of despair. Every man and every woman laboured to the uttermost for the defence of the city with a furious enthusiasm.

Two years after the siege began, **Publius Cornelius Scipio Africánus**, the Younger, was elected Consul while but thirty-seven (under the legal age), for the express purpose of giving him charge of the siege. After two years of desperate fighting and splendid heroism on the part of the defenders, the famished garrison could hold out no longer.

Carthage fell in 146, and the ruins of the city burned for seventeen days. The destruction was complete. A part of her territory was given to Numidia. The rest was made a Roman province, and called **Africa**.

The year 149 saw the death of two men who had been Carthage's

most bitter enemies, but who were not allowed to see her downfall,—
Masinissa and **Cato**, the one aged ninety, the other eighty-five.

Masinissa's (239-149) hostility dates from the time he failed to get the promised hand of Hasdrubal's daughter, Sophonisba, who was given to his rival, Syphax. After the Battle of Zama, most of the possessions of Syphax fell to Masinissa, and among them this same Sophonisba, whom he married. Scipio, however, fearing her influence over him, demanded her as a Roman captive, whereupon she took poison. Masinissa was a courageous prince, but a convenient tool for the Romans.

Cato the elder (*Major*), (234-149,) whose long public career was a constant struggle with the enemies of the state abroad, and with the fashions of his countrymen at home, was a type of the *old* Roman character, with a stern sense of duty that forbade his neglecting the interests of state, farm, or household. In 184, in his capacity as Censor, he acted with extreme rigor. He zealously asserted old-fashioned principles, and opposed the growing tendency to luxury. All innovations were in his eyes little less than crimes. He was the author of several works, one of which, a treatise on agriculture, has been preserved.

Cicero's "Cato Major" represents him in his eighty-fourth year discoursing about old age with Africánus the younger, and Laelius, a friend of the latter.

CHAPTER 20

Rome and Spain—The Numantine and Servile Wars (206-132)

Africánus the elder left Spain In 206. After a provincial government of nine years (206-197), The country was divided into two provinces, separated by the **Ibérus** (Ebro), and each province was assigned to a praetor. It was some time, however, before Spain was really brought into a state of complete peace and order. The mountains and forests were a formidable obstacle to the Roman legions, and favoured guerrilla warfare, which makes conquest slow and laborious.

The most warlike of the Spanish tribes was the **Celtibéri**, who occupied the interior of the peninsula. They were always uncertain and intractable, continually breaking out into revolt. In 195, Cato the elder put down a rebellion led by them. He established more firmly the Roman power east of the Ibérus. He disarmed the inhabitants of this part of Spain, and compelled all from the Pyrenees to the Guadalquivir to pull down their fortifications.

Still the smouldering fires of rebellion were not extinguished, for, sixteen years later (179), we find **Tiberius Sempronius Gracchus**, the father of the famous Gracchi, as Governor of Spain, fighting the troublesome Celtibéri. He captured over one hundred of their towns, but tempered his victories with moderate measures, showing himself greater in peace than in war. He granted to the poorer classes lands on favourable conditions, and did much to produce contentment among the natives. But farther west, in the valleys of the Douro and Tagus, and in Lusitania (Portugal), there seems to have been constant warfare.

In 154, **Mummius**, the same who eight years later sacked Corinth, was Governor of Farther Spain. His defeat by the Lusitanians encouraged the Celtibéri to revolt again, and there followed another defeat, with a massacre of many Roman citizens. Two years later (152), **Claudius Marcellus** avenged these losses, founded Corduba, and governed the country humanely. His successors, **Lucius Lucullus** and **Servius Galba**, were so cruel and grasping as to drive the Lusitanians into another open rebellion, headed by **Viriáthus**, a bold and daring bandit. During seven years (147-140) he defeated again and again the armies sent against him. The Celtibéri joined his standards, and Spain seemed likely to slip from the Romans. The only check to these successes was during the command of **Metellus Macedonicus** (143); when he was recalled, matters returned to their former condition.

In 140, the Consul Mancínus was obliged to capitulate, and, to save himself and his army, made a treaty which the Senate refused to sanction.

Viriáthus was finally (139) assassinated by persons hired by the Consul Caepio; his people were then subdued, and the government was ably conducted (138) by **Decimus Junius Brutus**.

THE NUMANTINE WAR (143-133).

The Celtibéri, however, were still in arms. The strong city of **Numantia**, the capital of one of their tribes, witnessed more than one defeat of a Roman Consul before its walls (141-140). Finally Rome sent out her best general, Africánus the younger.

After devoting several months to the disciplining of his troops, he began (134) a regular siege of the place. It was defended with the utmost bravery and tenacity, until, forced by the last extreme of famine, it surrendered (133). The inhabitants were sold as slaves, and the town was levelled to the ground. The victor was honored with the title of **Numantínus**.

The fall of Numantia gave Rome a hold upon the interior of Spain, which was never lost. The country now, with the exception of its northern coast, was nominally Roman territory. Several towns were established with Latin municipal rights (*municipia*), and, on the whole, order was maintained. Along the coast of the Mediterranean there sprang up many thriving and populous towns, which became centres of civilization to the neighbouring districts, and were treated by Rome rather as allies than as subjects. Some of them were allowed to coin the silver money of Rome. The civilizing process, due to Roman influence, went on rapidly in these parts, while the interior remained in barbarism.

In 105 the peninsula was overrun by the Cimbri, a barbarous race from the north. The country was ravaged, but finally saved by the brave Celtibéri, who forced the invaders back into Gaul.

THE SERVILE WAR (134–132).

While the Numantine war was still in progress, a war with the slaves broke out in Sicily, where they had been treated with special barbarity.

For a long-time slave labour had been taking the place of that of freemen. The supply was rendered enormous by constant wars, and by the regular slave-trade carried on with the shores of the Black Sea and Greece. The owners of the slaves became an idle aristocracy.

The immediate cause of the outbreak in Sicily was the cruelty of a wealthy slave-owner, Damophilus. The leader of the slaves was **Eunus**, who pretended to be a Syrian prophet. A number of defeats were suffered by the Roman armies, until, finally, **Publius Rutilius** captured the strongholds of the slaves, **Tauromenium** and **Enna**, and thus closed the war. For his success he was allowed an ovation.

CHAPTER 21

Internal History—The Gracchi

We have seen how the long struggle between the patricians and plebeians terminated in a nominal victory for the latter. From about 275, the outward form of the old constitution had undergone little change. It was nominally that of a "moderate democracy." The Senate and offices of state were, in law, open to all alike. In practice, however, the constitution became an oligarchy. The Senate, not the *Comitias*, ruled Rome. Moreover, the Senate was controlled by a class who claimed all the privileges of a nobility. The *Comitias* were rarely called upon to decide a question. Most matters were settled by a **Decree of the Senate** (*Senatus Consultum*). To be sure the *Comitia* declared for war or peace, but the Senate conducted the war and settled the conditions of peace. It also usually assigned the commands, organized the provinces, and managed the finances.

The causes for this ascendency of the Senate are not hard to find. It was a body made up of men capable of conducting affairs. It could be convened at any time, whereas the voters of the *Comitias* were scattered over all Italy, and, if assembled, would not be competent to decide questions demanding knowledge of military matters and foreign policy.

The Senate and the Roman nobility were in the main the same. All patricians were nobles, but all nobles were not patricians. The patricians were the descendants of the original founders of the city. The nobles were the descendants of anyone who had filled one of the following six *curule* offices, *viz*. Dictator, *Magister Equitum*, Consul, *Interrex*, *Praetor*, or *Curule Aedile*. These nobles possessed the right to place in their hall, or carry in funeral processions, a wax mask of this ancestor, and also of any other member of the family who had held a *curule* office.

A plebeian who first held this office was called a *novus homo*, or "new man."

The Senate, thus made up of patricians and nobles, had at this time the monopoly of power. Legally, however, it had no positive authority. The right of the people to govern was still valid, and there was only wanting a magistrate with the courage to remind them of their legal rights, and urge the exercise of them.

Such a magistrate was found in **Tiberius Sempronius Gracchus.** With him was ushered in the contest which lasted for more than a century, and brought to the surface some of the proudest names of Roman history. On one side or the other we find them,—**Marius** and **Sulla, Caesar** and **Augustus** and **Antony,**—arraying Rome against herself until the glories of the Republic were swallowed up in the misrule and dishonour of the Empire.

Tiberius Sempronius Gracchus the elder (see Chapter 20) belonged to the nobility, but not to the aristocracy. He married **Cornelia**, the daughter of Africánus the elder. They had twelve children, of whom all but three died young. Two sons and a daughter lived to maturity. The daughter, **Sempronia**, married Africánus the younger. The sons, **Tiberius** and **Gaius**, grew up under the care of their noble and gifted mother, who was left a widow when they were mere boys.

Tiberius (164-133) entered the army, and served under his brother-in-law during the third Punic war. Ten years later (136) he was *Quaestor* in Spain, where he won the affections of the people by adhering to the mild policy which his father had previously followed. His popular measures here displeased his brother-in-law, and he ceased to be a favourite with him. On his return home he passed through Tuscany where he was astonished to see large tracts of the *ager publicus* (see Chapter 7) cultivated by slave gangs, while the free poor citizens of the Republic were wandering in towns without employment, and deprived of the land which, according to law (see the Licinian Rogations), should have been divided among them, and not held in large quantities by the rich landowners.

Tiberius determined to rectify this wrong. In 133 he offered himself as candidate for the tribuneship, and was elected. He then began boldly the battle for the commons. He proposed to revise the Agrarian Law, now a dead letter, which forbade the holding of more than 320 acres of the *ager publicus* by one individual. Occupants who had fenced this land and improved it were to be compensated therefor.

The wealthy classes and the Senate at once took sides against Tiberius, and the struggle began. One of the other Tribunes, **Octavius Caecína**, who was himself a large landowner, taking advantage of his authority as Tribune, interposed his veto to prevent a vote upon the question. Gracchus, full of enthusiasm over the justice of his cause, obtained, contrary to all precedent, the removal of his colleague from office, and passed his Agrarian Law. Three commissioners were appointed, himself, his brother, and his father-in-law, **Appius Claudius**, to carry it into effect

It was contrary to the law that a person should hold the office of Tribune for two successive years. But Gracchus, in his desire to carry out his plans, determined to violate this rule, and offered himself as candidate for the next year. The election day came, and when it became evident that he would be re-elected, the aristocrats, who had turned out in full force on the Campus Martius with their retinues of armed slaves and clients, raised a riot, and, killing Gracchus with three hundred of his followers, threw their bodies into the Tiber (133). Thus was shed the first blood of the civil struggle. The mob was led by **Scipio Nasíca**, the uncle of Tiberius. Africánus, when he heard of the murder of his brother-in-law, exclaimed, "Justly slain."

The agrarian law, however, which had passed, was too evidently just to be openly ignored. The remaining two commissioners continued their work, until, within two years, 40,000 families were settled on tracts of the public land which the patricians were compelled to vacate. But the commissioners became unpopular, for those who received lands were not always satisfied, and those who were obliged to leave them were enraged. The commissioners were suspended, and the law repealed.

The mantle of Tiberius fell on **Gaius Gracchus**. For a time after his brother's death he retired from politics, and served in the army in Africa and Sardinia, where he was *Quaestor*. His valour, wisdom, and justice made him justly popular, but caused him to be regarded with suspicion at Rome. In 123 he was elected Tribune, and twice re-elected. He revived his brother's agrarian law, and became at once the avowed enemy of the Senate. As a means of increasing his popularity, he endeavoured to admit all the Italians to the privileges of Roman citizenship, and to limit the price of bread.

Gaius gained the favour of the *Equites* (Knights), the commercial class, by carrying through the assembly a law by which all judicial functions were taken from the Senate and intrusted to the Knights. Heretofore all civil and criminal cases of importance had been tried before a jury chosen from the Senate. These juries were often venal and corrupt, and it was a notorious fact that their verdicts could be bought.

The transferring of the juries to the *Equites* made Gaius for a time very powerful. He caused another law to be passed, to the effect that no Roman citizen should be put to death without legal trial and an appeal to the assembly of the people.

But the plan of Gaius to extend the franchise to all the Italians ruined his popularity. The Roman citizens had no desire to share their rights with the Etruscans and Samnites. Riots again broke out, as ten years before. The aristocracy again armed itself. Gaius with 3,000 of his friends was murdered in 121, and the Senate was once more master of the situation.

However, the results obtained by the Gracchi still remained. Forty thousand peasants had been settled on public land. The jury law was in force. No Roman citizen could be put to death without trial, unless the state was held to be in danger.

Nearly all Roman writers unite in attacking the reputation of the Gracchi; but viewed in the light of today their characters were noble, and their virtues too conspicuous to be obscured.

A few years previous to this, the younger Africánus died (129). His remark about the death of Tiberius Gracchus gave dire offence to the popular party, and a few days later he was found dead in his bed, probably "a victim of political assassination."

Africánus was a man of refinement and culture, a warm friend of scholars, a patron of the Greek historian **Polybius**, and of the poets **Lucilius** and **Terence**. He was opposed to the tendency of his age towards luxury and extravagance. He was an orator, as well as a general. The one blot on his career is the terrible destruction of Carthage, which he possibly might have averted had he shown firm opposition to it

Scipio Nasíca, who led the mob against Tiberius, was compelled, though Pontifex Maximus, to leave the city, and died an exile in Asia.

CHAPTER 22

External History—Pergamum—Jugurthine War (118-104)

Pergamum was an ancient city of Mysia on the Caícus, fifteen miles from the sea. It first became important after the death of Alexander. Its first king Attalus I. (241-197), added a large territory to the city. He was an ally of the Romans, and his successors remained their firm friends. The city became one of the most prosperous and famous in Asia Minor, noted for its architectural monuments, its fine library, and its schools. Attalus III., at his death in 133, bequeathed to Rome his kingdom which included Lydia, Pisidia, Lycaonia, and Pamphylia. It was made a province under the name of **Asia**.

THE WAR WITH JUGURTHA.

After the destruction of Carthage, the most important kingdom in Africa was **Numidia**. It contained a number of flourishing towns, which were centres of a considerable commerce. Masinissa left this kingdom to his son Micipsa. The latter had two sons and a nephew, **Jugurtha**. The nephew was a brilliant young man, who had served under Scipio in the Numantine war, and returned to Africa covered with honours. He was named joint heir with his cousins to the kingdom of Numidia. Micipsa dying soon after, Jugurtha murdered one of his cousins, Hiempsal, claimed the whole kingdom, and attacked his other cousin, Adherbal, who appealed to Rome. Commissioners were sent to investigate. They were bought off by Jugurtha, and returned home without accomplishing anything. Adherbal was afterwards captured, savagely tortured, and finally killed.

The Senate, compelled by the popular indignation to make an investigation, moved so slowly that some of its members were accused of accepting bribes. War was declared at last, but the campaign languished, and peace was soon made on such easy terms for the prince that it was evident his money had again been freely used. The scandalous transaction was denounced at Rome by the Tribune **Memmius**. Jugurtha then repaired to the city in person, and bought up all the authorities except Memmius, whom he found incorruptible. He had another cousin whom he caused to be murdered. After this the Senate ordered him to leave, and as he departed, it is said he exclaimed, "Venal city, destined soon to perish, if a purchaser be found!"

War was now begun in earnest (110), but resulted in a crushing defeat of the Romans, whose army was sent under the yoke. Humiliated by the defeat, the Senate in the following year sent **Quintus Caecilius Metellus**, nephew of Metellus Macedonicus, to take charge of the war. He was a man of integrity, with some experience as an officer, and a rigid aristocrat. Realizing the danger of failure, he took with him his lieutenant the ablest soldier that he could find, **Gaius Marius**.

Marius, born at Arpínum in 157, was the son of a farmer, and was himself bred to the plough. He joined the army at an early age, and soon attracted notice for his punctual performance of all duties, and his strictness in discipline. He was present at the siege of Numantia, and his courage caused Scipio to predict for him a brilliant career. He soon rose to be Military Tribune. In 119 he was chosen Tribune of the People, and two years later Praetor. The fact that he was respected and valued in high circles is shown by his subsequent marriage into the family of the Caesars. By this marriage with Julia, the aunt of Julius Caesar, he became a person of social distinction.

The campaign was moderately successful. Jugurtha was defeated near the River Muthul, and made to retire into the desert, where his stronghold, Thala, was captured. He sued for peace, but, as unconditional surrender was demanded, he still held out. The popular party at Rome, irritated that such a petty prince should give so much trouble, demanded that Marius should be made Consul and have charge of the war. When the lieutenant asked Metellus for leave of absence to enable him to be present at the elections, as was necessary according to the law, his general ridiculed the idea, and told him to wait another twenty years. He went, however, and was elected in 107, being the first plebeian chosen to that office for more than a century.

Metellus was recalled, enjoyed a triumph, and received the agnomen of **Numidicus**.

Marius was every inch a soldier. He saw that the Roman legions must be reorganized and better disciplined. He enlisted men who had no other occupation, that they might become professional soldiers. Some men of rank who had a taste for war also went with him. Among these was a young patrician, **Cornelius Sulla**. With this army Marius soon wrested from Jugurtha all his strongholds. In less than two years the war was over. By his ally, Bocchus, King of Mauritania, Jugurtha was betrayed (106) into the hands of Sulla, who was acting as the *Quaestor* of Marius.

The western portion of Numidia was given to Bocchus as the reward of his treachery, while the remainder continued to be governed by native princes, until the civil war between Caesar and Pompey. In 104 Marius returned home, and entered Rome in triumph. Jugurtha was thrown into a dungeon, and there starved to death.

CHAPTER 23

The Cimbri and Teutones—Political Quarrels

The war with Jugurtha ended none too soon, for Marius was needed in a struggle requiring all his talents.

The **Cimbri** and **Teutones**, barbarous nations from Northern Europe, were threatening the frontiers of Italy. Already the Roman armies had met with five successive defeats at their hands on the banks of the Rhone. Eighty thousand Romans and forty thousand camp followers are said to have fallen in these battles. Had the barbarians at this moment chosen to enter Italy, the destruction of Rome would have been a certain result. Fortunately, they turned to the Pyrenees, and, sweeping over the mountains, overran for a season the province of Spain.

Marius, appointed Consul a second time, devoted his energies to forming and training the army. He selected the plains on the banks of the Rhone in Southern Gaul as best adapted for his purpose. Here he drilled his troops, accustoming them to the greatest possible exertions. Many perished under the strain, but the survivors became hardened soldiers. Corps of engineers were attached to each legion, and the soldiers were taught the use of tools, as well as of arms. At length, in his fourth consulship (102), he felt prepared to meet the enemy.

The barbarians, on their return from Spain, separated their forces, the Cimbri marching around the northern foot of the Alps towards Noricum, with the intention of invading Italy from that quarter, while the Teutones remained in Gaul.

As the latter advanced, Marius took up his position in a fortified camp near **Aquae Sextiae** (Aix). He allowed the enemy to march past him, and then followed cautiously, waiting for a favourable opportunity to fall upon them. In the battle that followed, the barbarians were no match for the drilled legionaries, who were irresistible. The contest lasted two days, and the vast host of the Teutones was cut to pieces (20 July, 102). At the close of this battle word was brought to Marius that he had been elected Consul for the fifth time.

Meanwhile, the Cimbri had crossed the Alps and were ravaging the fertile fields of Lombardy, meeting with but slight opposition from Catulus, the other Consul.

The next year Marius came to his rescue. Near **Vercellae** the Cimbri met the same fate as their brethren, and Italy was saved (101).

No sooner was the danger from the invasion over than political quarrels broke out at Rome with great fury. Marius was elected Consul for the sixth time. The popular heroes of the hour were two demagogues, the Tribune **Saturnínus** and the Praetor **Glaucia**. They carried corn laws and land laws,[1] and compelled the Senators to take an oath to execute their laws. Metellus Numidicus refusing to comply with their wishes, Saturnínus sent a guard to the Senate-House, dragged him out, and expelled him from the city.

During this troublesome time, Marius showed that he was no politician. He lacked judgment and firmness, and by endeavouring to please all parties he pleased none.

On the popular side there were two parties, the moderate one, led by **Memmius**, who had exposed the Senate in its dealings with Jugurtha, and the radical one, led by Saturnínus and Glaucia. Memmius and Glaucia both ran for the consulship, and as the former seemed likely to be successful, he was murdered. A reaction then set in, and Saturnínus and Glaucia were declared public enemies. They took refuge in the Senate-House, the roof of which was torn off, and the wretches were stoned to death.

The fall of Saturnínus and Glaucia was followed in 99 by the recall of Metellus from banishment He died shortly afterwards, and it was suspected that he was a victim of treachery.

Marius having now become generally unpopular on account of his vacillating course in the recent troubles, went into voluntary exile,

---

1. These were the **Appuleian Laws** (100):—

1. Any Roman citizen could buy corn of the state at a nominal price.

2. The land in Cisalpine Gaul, which the Cimbrians had occupied, should be divided among the Italian and Roman citizens.

3. Colonies from the veterans of Marius were to be founded in Sicily, Achaia and Macedonia.

travelling through Asia Minor, and visiting the court of Mithradátes, King of Pontus.

For the next eight years (99-91) Rome enjoyed a season of comparative quiet.

CHAPTER 24

Internal History—The Social War (90-88)

At this time there was a bitter rivalry between the Senate and the equestrian order, or commercial class. From the former were chosen the governors of the provinces, from the latter came the tax-gatherers (*publicani*) and the money-brokers (*negotiatores*). It will help us to understand better the condition of affairs, if we study the composition of the Senate and the *Equites*.

The Senators, three hundred in number (later their number was increased to six hundred), held their office for life. When vacancies occurred from death, or occasionally from removal, they were filled by the Censor, [1] who appointed a person that had held one of the following offices: Dictator, Consul, *Praetor*, *Curule Aedile*, or, after the time of Sulla, *Quaestor*. All persons who had held these offices, or that of Tribune, were allowed to join in debate in the Senate, but not to vote. No Senator could engage in business. Hence he must be wealthy.

We saw in Chapter 4 that Roman citizens were divided into six classes according to their property, and that these classes were subdivided into one hundred and ninety-three other classes called centuries. About 225, the number was increased to three hundred and seventy-three. Eighteen, of the centuries of the first class were called **Equites**, and must have property worth twenty thousand dollars or more. This name was given to them because at first they served in the army as horsemen, though in later times the cavalry was composed only of allied troops. The *Equites* were originally from the aristocracy alone, but, as the plebeians increased in wealth, many of them became rich enough to be included in this class.

1. See the duties of Censor, Chapter 8.

There was no hostility between the Senate and the *Equites* until, in 123, Gaius Gracchus passed the *Lex Judicaria*, which prescribed that the jurors (*judices*) should be chosen from the *Equites*, and not the Senate. From this time dates the struggle between the two classes, and the breach widened every year. On the one side were the nobles, represented by the Senate; on the other side, the equestrian order.

Since the jurors were chosen from the latter, it had control of the courts, and often made an unscrupulous use of its power, especially in those courts which were established to try governors for extortion in the management of provinces (*quaestiones rerum repetundarum*). From the *Equites*, too, were taken the tax-gatherers of the provinces. They pillaged and robbed the people at will, and, if a governor had the courage to interfere with them, a threat of prosecution was held over his head. The average governor preferred to connive at their exactions; the bolder ones paid with fines or exiles for their courage.

Another trouble was threatening the commonwealth. The Italian allies of Rome did not possess the franchise belonging to a Roman citizen. For nearly two centuries they had shared dangers and victories with the Romans; they now eagerly demanded all their privileges.

In 91, **Marcus Livius Drusus**, the Tribune, took up the task of reform. He was noble, wealthy, and popular, and he hoped to settle the question peacefully and equitably. But his attempt to reform the courts displeased the *Equites*, his agrarian and corn laws made him many enemies, and his attempt to admit the Italians to the rights of Roman citizenship aroused great opposition.

His laws were passed, but the Senate pronounced them null and void. He was denounced in that body as a traitor, and was struck down by an assassin in the same year.

The death of Drusus drove the Italians to despair. Eight nations entered into a close alliance, chose **Corfinium**, in the Pelignian Apennines, as their capital, and formed a Federal Republic, to which they gave the name **Italia**. All Italians were to be citizens of Corfinium, and here was to be the place of assembly and the Senate-House.

Rome, in the face of this danger, acted promptly and with resolution. The Consuls, Lucius Julius Caesar and Publius Rutilius Lupus, both took the field; with each were five lieutenants, among whom were Marius and Sulla.

This war (90–88), called the **Social War**, *i. e.* the war with the allies (*Socii*), was at first disastrous to Rome. The allies overran Campania, defeated the Romans several times, and entered into negotiations with the Northern Italians, whose fidelity began to waver.

It is not strange, therefore, that opinions at Rome began to be turned in the direction of a more liberal policy. It was decided to make concessions. Towards the close of the year 90, the Consul Caesar carried the **Julian Law**, by which the Roman franchise was extended to all who had not yet revolted. The next year this law was supplemented by the **Plautian Papirian Law**, which allowed every citizen of an Italian town the franchise, if he handed in his name to the Praetor at Rome within sixty days. About the same time was passed another law, the **Calpurnian**, which permitted Roman magistrates in the field to bestow the franchise on all who wished it. These laws resulted in disorganizing the rebellion. The Samnites and Lucanians held out the longest, but were finally put down by Marius.

The end of the Social War brought no peace at Rome. The newly enfranchised Italians were not fully satisfied. The Senate was torn asunder by violent personal rivalries. There was no class not affected by the wide-spread tightness in the money market The treasury was empty, and many capitalists became insolvent War with Mithradátes, King of Pontus, had been declared, and both Marius and Sulla were eager to have the command.

At this time (88) the Tribune **Publius Sulpicius Rufus** brought forward the following bills:—

1. That the command of the war against Mithradátes be given to Marius.

2. That the new citizens should be distributed through all the tribes.

3. That any Senator who owed more than four hundred dollars be deprived of his seat

4. That those exiled on suspicion of having aided in the Italian revolt be recalled.

In spite of the bitterest opposition, these bills were passed. But the triumph of Sulpicius was of short duration. Sulla, who with his troops had been encamping near Nola in Campania, marched upon the city, and for the first time a Consul entered Rome at the head of his legions.

CHAPTER 25

Marius And Sulla—Cinna

With the name of **Marius** is usually coupled that of **Lucius Cornelius Sulla** (138-78).

"He was a patrician of the purest blood, had inherited a moderate fortune, and had spent it, like other young men of rank, lounging in theatres and amusing himself with dinner parties. He was a poet, an artist, and a wit Although apparently indolent, he was naturally a soldier, statesman, and diplomatist. As *Quaestor* under Marius in the Jugurthine War, he had proved a most active and useful officer."

In these African campaigns he showed that he knew how to win the hearts and confidence of his soldiers; and through his whole subsequent career, the secret of his brilliant successes seems to have been the enthusiastic devotion of his troops, whom he always held well under control, even when they were allowed to indulge in plunder and license. It was to Sulla's combined adroitness and courage that Marius owed the final capture of Jugurtha. He served again under Marius in the campaigns against the Cimbri and Teutones, and gave efficient help towards the victory. But the Consul became jealous of his rising power, and all friendly feeling between the two ceased.

After this campaign Sulla lived at Rome for some years, taking no part in politics, and during this time his name and that of his rival are almost unheard. He appeared before the public again in 93, when he was elected *Praetor*, and increased his popularity by an exhibition of a hundred lions in the arena, matched against Numidian archers. In 92 he went as *Propraetor* to govern the province of Asia, and here he first met **Mithradátes**.

This monarch, who ruled over Pontus, was an extraordinary man. He spoke many languages, was the idol of his subjects, and had boundless ambition. He doubted the durability of the Roman Empire, and began to enlarge his own territory, with no apparent fear of Rome's interference.

Cappadocia, a neighbouring country, was under Roman protection, and was ruled by a prince, **Ariobarzánes**, that Rome had recognized. This country Mithradátes attacked. He killed the prince, and placed on the throne his own nephew.

Rome interfered, and Sulla was instructed to visit the monarch. He accomplished his mission with his usual adroitness, and returned to Rome with new honours. He took an active part in the Social War, eclipsing the fame of his rival, Marius. He was now the recognized leader of the conservative and aristocratic party. The feeling between the rivals was more bitter than ever, for Marius, though old, had by no means lost his prestige with the popular party.

It was at this time that Mithradátes, learning of the Social War, thought it a good opportunity to advance his own interests and extend his realm. He collected all his available forces, and invaded Bithynia. With his fleets he sailed through the Dardanelles into the Archipelago. The extortions of the Roman governors had been sp great, that Ionia, Lydia, and Caria, with all the islands near Asia Minor, gladly revolted from Rome, and accepted his protection. All the Roman residents with their families were massacred on a single day. It is said that 80,000 persons perished. Mithradátes himself next crossed the Bosphorus, and marched into Northern Greece, which received him with open arms.

Such was the condition in the East when Sulpicius Rufus carried the bills mentioned in the last chapter. One of these bills was that Marius have charge of the war against Mithradátes. This was not to Sulla's liking. He was, in Campania with the legions that had served in the Social War. The soldiers were devoted to him, and ready to follow him anywhere. Sulla, therefore, taking matters into his own hands, marched into the city at the head of his troops. The people resisted; Sulpicius was slain; Marius fled for his life, and retired to Africa, where he lived for a time, watching the course of events.

Sulla could not remain long at the capital. The affairs of the East called him away; and no sooner was he gone than the flames of civil war burst out anew (87).

Lucius Cornelius Cinna, a friend of Marius, was Consul that year. He tried to recall Marius, but was violently opposed and finally driven from the city. The Senate declared him deposed from his office. He invoked the aid of the soldiers in Campania, and found them ready to follow him. The neighbouring Italian towns sent him men and money, and Marius, coming from Africa, joined him with six thousand troops. They marched upon Rome. The city was captured. Cinna was acknowledged Consul, and the sentence of outlawry which had been passed on Marius was revoked.

The next year Marius was made Consul for the seventh time, and Cinna for the second. Then followed the wildest cruelties. Marius had a bodyguard of slaves, which he sent out to murder whomever he wished. The houses of the rich were plundered, and the honour of noble families was exposed to the mercy of the slaves. Fortunately Marius died sixteen days after he entered office, and the shedding of blood ceased.

For the next three years Cinna ruled Rome. Constitutional government was practically suspended. For the years 85 and 84 Cinna himself and a trusty colleague were Consuls, but no regular elections were held. In 84, he was murdered, when on the eve of setting out against Sulla in Asia.

Sulla left Italy for the East with 30,000 troops. He marched against Athens, where Archeláus, the general of Mithradátes, was intrenched. After a long siege, he captured and pillaged the city, March 1, 86. The same year he defeated Archeláus at **Chaeronéa** in Boeotia, and the next year at **Orchomenos**.

Meanwhile Sulla's lieutenant, **Lucullus**, raised a fleet and gained two victories off the coast of Asia Minor. The Asiatic king was now ready to negotiate. Sulla crossed the Hellespont in 84, and in a personal interview with the king arranged the terms of peace, which were as follows. The king was to give up Bithynia, Paphlagonia, and Cappadocia, and withdraw to his former dominions. He was also to pay an indemnity amounting to about $3,500,000, and surrender eighty ships of war.

Having thus settled matters with the king, Sulla punished the Lydians and Carians, in whose territory the Romans had been massacred, by compelling them to pay at one time five years' tribute. He was now ready to return to Rome.

The same year that Cinna died, Sulla landed at Brundisium, with 40,000 troops and a large following of nobles who had fled from Rome. Every preparation was made by the Marian party for his reception; but no sooner did he land in Italy than the soldiers were induced to desert to him in immense numbers, and he soon found himself in possession of all Lower Italy. Among those who hastened to his standard was young **Pompey**, then but twenty-three years old, and it was to his efforts that Sulla's success was largely due.

The next year, 83, the Marian party was joined by the Samnites, and the war raged more fiercely than ever. At length, however, Sulla was victorious under the walls of Rome. The city lay at his mercy. His first act, an order for the slaughter of 6,000 Samnite prisoners, was a fit prelude to his conduct in the city. Every effort was made to eradicate the last trace of Marian blood and sympathy from city. A list of men, declared to be outlaws and public enemies, was exhibited in the Forum, and a succession of wholesale murders and confiscations throughout Rome and Italy, made the name of Sulla forever infamous.

Having received the title of Dictator, and celebrated a splendid triumph for the Mithradátic war, he carried (80-79) his political measures. The main object of these was to invest the Senate, the thinned ranks of which he filled with his own creatures, with full control over the state, over every magistrate and every province.

In 79 he resigned his dictatorship and went to Puteoli, where he died the next year, from a loathsome disease brought on by his excesses.

THE REFORMS OF SULLA.

Sulla restricted the power of the magistrates to the advantage of the Senate. Senators were alone made eligible for the tribuneship, and no former Tribune could hold any *curule* office. No one could be *Praetor* without having first been *Quaestor*, or Consul without having held the *praetorship*. Every candidate for the office of *Quaestor* must be at least thirty years old. The number of *Praetors* was increased from six to eight; that of *Quaestors*, from twelve to twenty. The Consuls and *Praetors* were to remain at Rome during their first year of office, and then go to the provinces as Proconsuls and *Propraetors*.

Three hundred new Senators, taken from the *Equites*, were added, and all who had been *Quaestors* were made eligible to the Senate. The control of the courts was transferred from the *Equites* to the Senate.

On the death of Sulla, in 78, **Crassus** and **Lepidus** were chosen Consuls; but such was the instability of the times that they were sworn not to raise an army during their consulship. Lepidus attempted to evade his oath by going to Gaul, and, when summoned by the Senate to return, marched against the city at the head of his forces. He was defeated by Crassus and Pompey in 78, and soon after died.

CHAPTER 26

Sertorius—Spartacus—Lucullus—Pompey And Crassus

Quintus Sertorius (121-72), a native of the little Sabine village of Nursia under the Apennines, had joined the party of Marius, and served under him in the campaigns against the Cimbri and Teutones. In 97 he served in Spain, and became acquainted with the country with which his fame is chiefly associated. In 91 he was Quaestor in Cisalpine Gaul. He was a partisan of Marius during his troubles with Sulla, and on Sulla's return from the East he left Rome for Spain, where he took the lead of the Marian party. His bravery, kindness, and eloquence pleased the Spaniards. Many Roman refugees and deserters joined him. He defeated one of Sulla's generals, and drove out of Lusitania (Portugal) **Metellus Pius**, [1] who had been specially sent against him from Rome.

The object of Sertorius was to establish a government in Spain after the Roman model. He formed a Senate of three hundred members, and founded at Osca a school for native children. He was strict and severe towards his soldiers, but kind to the people. A white fawn was his favourite pet and constant follower. He ruled Spain for six years.

In 77 he was joined by **Perperna**, a Roman officer. The same year Pompey, then a young man, was sent to co-operate with Metellus. Sertorius proved more than a match for both of these generals, and defeated them near Saguntum.

The position of the Romans was becoming critical, for Sertorius

---

1. Son of Metellus Numidicus. He received the agnomen of Pius on account of the love which he displayed for his father, whom he begged the people to recall from banishment in 99.

now formed a league with the pirates of the Mediterranean. He also entered into negotiations with Mithradátes, and opened correspondence with the slaves in Italy, who were rebelling.

But intrigues and jealousies arose in his camp. The outcome of these was that he was treacherously murdered by Perperna at a banquet in 72, and with his death fell the Marian party in Spain.

Meanwhile a dangerous enemy was threatening Italy within her own borders. In 73 a band of gladiators, under the leadership of one of their number, named **Spartacus**, escaped from the training school at Capua and took up a strong position on Mount Vesuvius. They were joined by large numbers of slaves and outcasts of every description, and were soon in a position to defeat two *Praetors* who were sent against them.

The next year they assumed the offensive; and Spartacus found himself at the head of 100,000 men. Four generals sent against him were defeated; and for two years he ravaged Italy at will, and even threatened Rome. But intestine division showed itself in his ranks; his lieutenants grew jealous of him, and his strength began to wane.

In 71 the command of the war was given to **Crassus**, who finished it in six months. Spartacus fell, fighting bravely, near Brundisium. Pompey, returning from the Sertorian war in Spain, met five thousand of those who had escaped from the army of Spartacus. These he slew to a man. Crassus pointed the moral of his victory by hanging, along the road from Rome to Capua, six thousand captives whom he had taken.

Mithradátes meanwhile, taking advantage of the troubles at Rome, was again in arms, and in 74 **Lucius Licinius Lucullus** was sent against him.

Lucullus, of plebeian birth, first distinguished himself in the Social War, where he gained the favour of Sulla, and accompanied him, as *Quaestor*, in his campaign against Mithradátes in 88. With Cotta he was chosen to the consulship in 74. The province of Cilicia was assigned to him, Bithynia to Cotta. Mithradátes invaded Bithynia, defeated Cotta, and besieged him at Chalcédon.

Lucullus, after reorganizing and disciplining his army, went to the aid of his colleague, drove the king into Pontus, and defeated him at Cabíra in 72, and his fleet at Tenedos in 71, compelling him to take refuge with his son-in-law, **Tigránes**, King of Armenia.

Lucullus endeavoured to work reforms in the administration of provincial governments in the East. The revenues of the provinces were farmed out, and the measures of Lucullus were intended to protect the tax-payers against the tax-gatherers (*publicani*). His reforms met with bitter opposition at Rome, especially from the *Equites*, whose chief source of income was often this same tax-farming. Intrigues against him by persons sent from Rome began to create dissatisfaction among his troops. He had been a severe disciplinarian, and so it was all the easier to turn the soldiers against him.

In 68 he won a victory over Tigránes and Mithradátes, at the River Arsanias; but his legions refused to follow him farther, and he was obliged to lead them into winter quarters in Mesopotamia. The next year his soldiers again mutinied, and he was replaced by Pompey.

Returning to Rome, Lucullus spent the rest of his days in retirement, dying about 57. He was very rich, and was famed for the luxurious dinners which he gave.

Pompey and Crassus.

The Sullan system stood for nine years, and was then overthrown, as it had been established, by a soldier. It was the fortune of Pompey, a favourite officer of Sulla, to cause the first violation of the laws laid down by his general.

Gneius Pompeius Magnus (106-48) led a soldier's life from his boyhood to his death. When a youth of seventeen he fought by his father's side in the civil struggles between Marius and Sulla. He was a partisan of the latter, and connected himself with the cause of the aristocracy. He defeated the followers of Marius in Sicily and Africa, and in 81 was allowed to enjoy a triumph, though still an *Eques* and not legally qualified. Sulla then greeted him with the surname of Magnus, which he ever afterwards bore. He was then sent to Spain, with what success we have seen in the previous chapter. In 70 Pompey and **Marcus Licinius Crassus** were elected Consuls amid great enthusiasm.

Crassus (108-53), the conqueror of Spartacus, had amassed immense wealth by speculation, mining, dealing in slaves, and other methods. Avarice is said to have been his ruling passion, though he gave large sums to the people for political effect.

Neither Pompey nor Crassus, according to the laws passed by Sulla, was eligible to the consulship. The former had never been *Quaestor*, and was only thirty-five years old; the latter was still Praetor, and ought to have waited two years.

The work of Sulla was now quickly undone. The Tribunes regained their prerogative, the veto. The control of the criminal courts was transferred again from the Senate to the Equites, and the former body was cleared of its most worthless members, who had been appointed by Sulla.

For three years (70-67) after the expiration of his consulship, Pompey remained quietly at Rome. He was then put in charge of an expedition against the Greek pirates. From the earliest times these marauders had been in the habit of depredating on the shores of the Mediterranean. During the civil wars of Rome they had become much bolder, so that the city was compelled to take an active part against them. They had paralyzed the trade of the Mediterranean, and even the coasts of Italy were not safe from their raids.

Gabinius, a Tribune, proposed that Pompey should hold his command for three years; that he should have supreme authority over all Roman magistrates in the provinces throughout the Mediterranean, and over the coasts for fifty miles inland. He was to have fifteen lieutenants, all ex-*praetors*, two hundred ships, and all the troops he needed.

In three months the pirates were swept from the sea.

The next year (66) Pompey's powers were still further enlarged by the **Manilian Law**, proposed by the Tribune Manilius. By this law the entire control of the Roman policy in the East was given to Pompey. His appointment was violently opposed by the Senate, especially by **Catulus**, the "father of the Senate," and by the orator **Hortensius**; but Cicero with his first political speech (*Pro Lege Manilia*) came to Pompey's assistance, and to him was given the command by which he became virtually dictator in the East. His operations there were thoroughly successful, and, though he doubtless owed much to the previous victories of Lucullus, he showed himself an able soldier. Mithradátes was obliged to flee across the Black Sea to Panticapaeum (Kertch).

In the year 64 Pompey went to Syria, took possession of the country in the name of Rome, and made it a province.

Next he was invited to act as judge between Hyrcánus and Aristobúlus, two aspirants to the Jewish throne. His decision was contrary to the wishes of the people, and to enforce it he led his army against Jerusalem, which he captured after a siege of three months. He installed Hyrcánus on the throne on condition of an annual tribute.

Meanwhile Mithradátes had returned to Pontus for the prosecution of his old design; but so great was the terror inspired by the Roman arms, that even his own son refused to join him. Desperate at the turn affairs had taken the aged monarch put an end to his own life in

63, after a reign of fifty-seven years. With him ceased for many years all formidable opposition to Rome in Asia.

Besides Syria, Pontus, to which Bithynia was joined, and Crete were now made provinces. Cilicia was reorganized, and enlarged by the addition of Pamphylia and Isauria. The three countries in Asia Minor not yet provinces, dependencies, were Galatia, ruled by Deiotarus; Cappadocia, by Ariobarzánes; and Paphlagonia, by Attalus.

After an absence of nearly seven years, Pompey returned January 1, 61, and enjoyed a well earned triumph. He was forty-five years old, had accomplished a really great work, had founded several cities which afterwards became centres of Greek life and civilization, and was hailed as the conqueror of Spain, Africa, and Asia.

The rest of Pompey's life is closely connected with that of Caesar. His wife, Julia, was Caesar's daughter, and thus far the relations between the two men had been friendly.

Pompey's absence in the East was marked at Rome by the rise to political importance of **Caesar** and **Cicero**, and by the conspiracy of **Catiline**.

CHAPTER 27

Caesar—Cicero—Verres

The Caesars were a family belonging to the Julian *gens*, which claimed descent from **Iúlus**, the son of **Aenéas**. Eight generations of Caesars had held prominent places in the commonwealth. They had been Consuls, Praetors, Censors, Aediles, and were aristocrats of the moderate wing. The direct ancestry of **Gaius Julius Caesar** can be traced no further back than his grandfather. This gentleman, of the same name as the great Caesar, married Marcia, who claimed descent from Ancus Marcius, the fourth King of Rome. They had three children, Gaius Julius, the father of the Dictator, Sextus Julius, and Julia, who became the wife of Marius. Gaius Julius held no higher office than Praetor. He was married to Aurelia, a stately woman of simple and severe tastes. Their son Gaius was born on July 12th, 100.

During Cinna's consulship (86), Caesar is first mentioned as a youth, tall, slight, handsome, with dark, piercing eyes, sallow complexion, and features refined and intellectual The bloody scenes attending the proscription of his uncle Marius, to whose party his father belonged, must have made a deep impression upon him. One of his most intimate companions was Cicero, who was six years his senior.

Marius had seen in his nephew the materials which make great men, and determined to help him to promotion. He made him, when scarcely fifteen, a priest of Jupiter (*flamen dialis*), which sacred office carried with it a handsome income.

Shortly after the death of his father, in 84, Caesar married Cornelia, the daughter of Cinna. By this marriage he was connected more closely with the popular party, whose champion he remained.

When Sulla returned to Rome from his Eastern campaign, Caesar was but eighteen. In the wholesale murders that followed, his party was ruined, his nearest friends dispersed or killed. He himself was yet free from proscription, for Sulla wished to win such a promising young man to his own side. He made proposals that Caesar divorce his wife and marry one whom he might select Caesar refused. Force was then tried. His priesthood was taken from him, and his wife's dowry. His estate was confiscated, and, when this had no effect, he was himself declared an outlaw, and a price was set on his head. Influential friends, however, interceded in his behalf, and the Dictator was finally persuaded to pardon him; but with reluctance, and with the remark that in Caesar was the making of many a Marius. The youth then left Italy, and joined the army in Asia.

Here Caesar served his apprenticeship as a soldier. He joined the forces of the Praetor Thermus, who had been the pirates that were making their headquarters in Lesbos. The *Praetor*, finding his troops insufficient to accomplish his work, sent Caesar to Nicomédes, a Roman ally and the King of Bithynia, to obtain additional forces. He was successful in his mission, and, upon his return to Lesbos, distinguished himself for his bravery in the attack upon Mityléne, and was awarded the oak wreath, a coveted honour, for saving the life of a fellow-soldier.

Caesar is next seen in Cilicia, serving under Servilius, in a campaign against the pirates who were marauding along the coast of that country. While here he was informed of Sulla's death, and at once left the army and returned home (77). The next year he began his struggle with the nobility by prosecuting for extortion Dolabella, a former Governor of Macedonia. Dolabella was a favourite of the Senate, and his cause was theirs. The best talent was engaged to defend him, and Caesar lost the case.

Feeling his deficiency as an orator, Caesar went to Rhodes and studied rhetoric under the famous Apollonius. He had recovered his property and priesthood, and could well afford the time. While on his way he was captured by pirates, and not released until a ransom of some $50,000 was raised and paid. Upon arriving at Milétus he at once got together some vessels, returned to the island where he had been in captivity, seized the crew of pirates, took them to Pergamus, and had them tried, convicted, and crucified. He then resumed his journey to Rhodes, where he remained two years in the pursuit of his studies. Then the report of the uprisal of Mithradátes reached him, and he at once crossed over to the mainland, collected a body of volunteers, and saved Caria to Rome.

Having finished his studies, Caesar returned to Rome and lived quietly for a time with his wife and mother, watching the course of events.

While Caesar was thus preparing himself for the great struggle in which he was destined to take the leading part, Cicero, the companion of his youth, was beginning to attract attention at Rome.

Marcus Tullius Cicero (106-43) was a townsman of Marius. He belonged to the Equites, and received a good education under the best Greek teachers. As he ripened into manhood, he chose in politics the party opposed to Caesar, and for a profession he selected the bar, hoping to gain fame as a speaker before the Senate, and finally to become one of its members. He took part in the Social War (89), but during the troubled times that followed he remained quietly engaged in literary pursuits. His first public oration (80), the defence of Roscius, who was falsely accused of murdering his father, was a great success, and guaranteed for him a brilliant future. Cicero improved the next few years by study and travel in Asia and Greece. Shortly after his return, in 75, he was elected *Quaestor*, and thus became a member of the Senate. His year of office he spent in Sicily, in the performance of his duties. There he obtained an insight into the corrupt extortions of the Roman governors. Five years later, he conducted his famous case against Verres.

Verres had been a follower of Sulla, and during the proscriptions had amassed some property. Afterwards he held official positions in Greece and Asia, where he became notorious for his greediness and cruelty. With the money thus acquired, he had bought his election to the *praetorship*, became Senator, and was sent by his colleagues to govern Sicily. His government there may have been no worse than that of many other proconsuls in the different provinces, but we have a fuller account of it owing to the prosecution of Cicero, whose speeches against Verres are preserved.

Verres was Governor of Sicily for three years. In his official position, he was judge of all civil and criminal cases. Every suit brought before him he gave to the party that could pay him best. Property was confiscated on false charges, and works of art of great value were stolen. By such a course Verres collected, it is said, property to the value of $4,000,000. Two thirds of this he expected to spend in silencing accusations. The rest he hoped to enjoy in peace, but Cicero's eloquence forced him to abandon his defence and retire into exile.

It was about this time that Caesar finished his rhetorical studies abroad, and returned home. He was elected Military Tribune as a reward for what he had accomplished in Caria. Two years later, in 68, he was elected *Quaestor*, thereby acquiring a seat in the Senate. At this time his Aunt Julia died, and, as one of her nearest relatives, he delivered the funeral oration.

Caesar was now beginning to know Pompey, and saw that their interests were common. The latter, although but six years older, was already a great man and a distinguished soldier. Cornelia, Caesar's wife, died, and he married for a second wife Pompeia, the cousin of Pompey. When sent as *Quaestor* to Farther Spain, in 67, he completed the work begun by Pompey and settled the finances of the troubled country, a task which he found the easier as he was known to belong to the popular party, of which Marius and Sertorius had been leaders.

CHAPTER 28

Troubles at Rome—Conspiracy of Catiline

While Pompey was absent in the East, matters at Rome were daily becoming worse, and shaping themselves for the speedy overthrow of the Republic. There were many who had suffered under Sulla, and who were anxious to regain what they had lost, and there were many who, enriched by the Dictator, had squandered their ill-gotten wealth, and now only waited a leader to renew the assault upon the state. The Senate was jealous of the power of the people distrusted the Senate.

Among the patricians who were aspiring to the consulship was **Lucius Sergius Catilína**, a villain steeped in every crime, but adroit, bold, and withal captivating. In 68 he had been *Praetor*, the next year Governor in Africa, where by his extortions he had obtained enough money, as he hoped, to purchase his election to the consulship. On his return home he was impeached for his misgovernment, but acquitted through Cicero's defence and the careful selection of a jury.

He then came forward as candidate for the consulship of the next year (63). There were two other candidates, Antonius, the uncle of Mark Antony, and Cicero himself. Antony was sure of an election, so the struggle was really between Catiline and Cicero. The latter was elected, owing to the popularity he had acquired by his prosecution of Verres and his defence of the Manilian Law. Thus Cicero reached the goal for which he had been so long striving.

Caesar was rising at the same time. The year previous (65) he had been *Curule Aedile*, had built a row of costly columns in front of the Capitol, and erected a temple to the Dioscúri (Castor and Pollux). But what made him especially pleasing to the populace was his lavish display at the public games and exhibitions.

Caesar was now looked upon as a prominent democratic leader. In 63 the office of Pontifex Maximus, the head of the state religion, became vacant by the death of its occupant, Metellus Pius. Caesar became a candidate for the office, and was elected, receiving more votes than both the rival candidates combined. He also received further evidence of the popular favour by being chosen Praetor for the next year (62).

Cicero's consulship would have closed without adding anything to his fame had it not been for Catiline. The latter's failure to be elected caused him to enter into a plot to seize and burn the city. He had many followers, men of noble families, among whom were the former Consul Lentulus, who had been recently expelled from the Senate by the Censors, and Cethégus, a bankrupt spendthrift, who was anxious to regain a fortune by a change in government. There were veterans of Sulla, starving peasants who had been dispossessed of their farms, and outlaws of every description. The conspirators were divided into two parties; those outside of the city, headed by Marcus Manlius, whose headquarters were at Faesulae (Fiesole), where was gathered an army of trained soldiers; and those inside of the city, headed by Catiline. Here secret meetings were held, the purpose of which was to excite an uprising, kill the magistrates, seize the government, and then unite with the army in Etruria. Cicero was informed of these meetings by spies, and just before the plans for the uprising were matured, he disclosed them to the Senate.

Catiline fled from Rome; but his accomplices, of whom Lentulus and Cethégus were the most prominent, were arrested in the city. A serious difficulty now arose as to the disposition of the prisoners. Lentulus was at that time *Praetor*, and the persons of public officers were sacred. The Sempronian Law of Gracchus forbade the executing of any Roman citizen without giving him a right of appeal to the Assembly. Too many were implicated in the conspiracy for this to be safe.

In the debate in the Senate, the principal speakers were Caesar, Cato, and Cicero.

Cato and Cicero advocated immediate death; Caesar, imprisonment for life. The motives of the men are so characteristic that they form a complete key to their several public careers. Cicero, vain and selfish, weak in council, and distrustful of the temper of the people and of his own ability to rule their factions, feared that they would become dangerous enemies to himself; Cato, desiring the reformation of the state, would make an example and warning for the future. The one, forgetful of the state, was overcome by personal fears; the other, unmindful of self, would have purity at any cost.

Caesar on the other hand, wished everything done in strict accordance with the laws; as a bold and wise statesman, he urged that nothing was more impolitic than lawless violence on the part of the rulers. Cicero was the timid magistrate; Cato, the injudicious reformer; but Caesar, with his keener knowledge and stronger hand, was the safer guide.

A sentence of death was voted; and Cicero, with unseemly haste, caused the conspirators to be strangled that same night (December 5, 63). The suppression of the conspiracy in the city was followed by the defeat of the army in Etruria. Thither Catiline had fled, and there he fell fighting with desperate courage at the head of his motley force of soldiers near Pistoria.

The name of "Father of his Country" was given to Cicero for the vigilance shown in this affair.

The execution of Lentulus and Cethégus resulted as Caesar had expected. It was a lawless act on the part of the Consul and the Senate, and it was felt that by it the constitution was still more endangered. The people demanded that Pompey return. In him they thought to have a deliverer from internal strifes.

Cicero was wrapped up in his own conceit, imagining himself a second Romulus. On the last day of the year (63), as was the custom of the retiring Consuls, he arose in the Forum to deliver a speech, reviewing the acts of his year of consulship. Metellus Nepos, a Tribune, forbade his speaking, on the ground that one who had put to death Roman citizens without a hearing did not deserve to be heard. Amid the uproar Cicero could only shout that he had saved his country. Metellus threatened to impeach him, and excitement in the city was at fever heat. The Tribune moved before the Assembly that Pompey be recalled. The Senate feared his coming. Caesar, who was now *Praetor* (judge), favoured it, and earnestly seconded the proposal of Metellus. Cato, who was also Tribune, ordered Metellus to stop speaking, and snatched his manuscript from his hand.

The aristocrats drew their swords, and broke up the meeting. Constitutional law was trampled underfoot on all sides. The Senate was riding rough-shod over all opponents. Metellus and Caesar were declared deposed from their offices. The people, however, believed in Caesar. He was followed to his home by crowds, who begged him to be their leader, and make an example of the law-breakers in the Senate. But

Caesar refused. He would have nothing to do with lawlessness; he let his opponents play that *rôle*, and awaited the results. The Senate soon saw its mistake, and requested him to resume his official duties.

The next year (61) Caesar was sent to Farther Spain as *Propraetor*. He had already left a favourable impression there as *Quaestor*. Portions of the country were still unsubdued. Many of the mountain passes were held by robbers, whose depredations caused much trouble. He completed the subjugation of the peninsula, put down the brigands, reorganized the government, and sent large sums of money to the treasury at Rome. His administration was thorough and complete, and a just reward for it would, he hoped, be the consulship.

Meanwhile Pompey had returned from the East. He landed at Brundisium in December, 62, and proceeded with a large band of captured princes and immense treasures to Rome, which he entered in triumph amidst the greatest enthusiasm. By a special vote of the Senate he was permitted to wear his triumphal robe in that body whenever he pleased.

Caesar returned from Spain in 60, with wealth and military fame. Though feared and detested by the Senate, he was the favourite of the people, and could depend upon their support Pompey had the army behind him. He received Caesar with pleasure, for he had been a friend in all his career.

Caesar felt that, with the people and the army through Pompey on his side, he only needed the capitalists to make his success sure. **Crassus** was counted as the richest man at Rome. He was won over. These three then formed what is known as the **First Triumvirate**,— "a union of shrewdness, renown, and riches," by which Caesar expected to rise to great power, Pompey to retain his power, and Crassus to gain greater wealth.

CHAPTER 29

The First Triumvirate

Pompey was ostensibly at the head of the first *Triumvirate*, and in return supported Caesar in his candidacy for the consulship. Crassus was to contribute his wealth to influence the election. Caesar was elected without opposition (59); his colleague, the Senate's tool, was Marcus Bibulus.

Caesar had now reached the highest round in the ladder of political offices. He had shown himself in all his course to be careful in keeping within the bounds of the constitution, never exerting himself in political quarrels except to defend the law against lawlessness. Now he was in a position to push his ideas of reform, and to show the aristocracy of what stuff he was made.

It would have been well for Cicero, and better for the state, had the orator been willing to join hands with Caesar and Pompey; but he was too vain of his own glory to join hands with those who were his superiors, and he clung to the Senate, feeling that his talents would shine there more, and be more likely to redound to his own personal fame.

Caesar's consulship increased his popularity among all except the aristocrats. His **Agrarian Law**, carefully framed and worded, was bitterly opposed by the Senate, especially by his colleague Bibulus, and by Cato. The law provided that large tracts of the *ager publicus*, then held on easy terms by the rich patricians, be distributed among the veterans of Pompey. Caesar proposed to pay the holders a reasonable sum for their loss, though legally they had no claim whatever on the land. Although Bibulus interfered, Cato raved, and the Tribunes vetoed, still the Assembly passed the law, and voted in addition that the Senate be obliged to take an oath to observe it.

The **Leges Juliae** were a code of laws which Caesar drew up during his year of office. They mark an era in Roman law, for they cover many crimes the commission of which had been for a long time undermining the state.

The most important of these was the **Lex de Repetundis**, aimed at the abuses of governors of provinces. It required all governors to make a double return of their accounts, one to be left in the province open for inspection, the other to be kept at Rome.

When Caesar's term of office was nearly ended, he obtained from the reluctant Senate his appointment as Pro-consul of Gaul for five years. He must leave the city, however, in safe hands, otherwise all his work would be undone. He managed the consular elections for the next year (58) so adroitly, that Piso and Gabinius, on whose friendship he could rely, were elected.

There were in Rome, however, two men whom it would be dangerous for Caesar to leave behind. Cato, the ultra aristocrat, hated him bitterly. Cicero, whose ambition was to lead the Senate, a body only too willing to crush Caesar, might do him great harm. It was Caesar's good fortune, or, as some believe, the result of his own scheming, that both these men were put temporarily out of the way.

Clodius Pulcher was a young aristocrat, notorious for his wildness. At one time, by assuming the dress of a woman, he had gained admittance to the festival of *Bona Dea*, which was celebrated only by women. He was discovered and brought to trial before the Senate, but acquitted by means of open bribery. Cicero had been instrumental in bringing him to trial, and Clodius never forgot it. He got adopted into a plebeian family in order to be a candidate for the tribuneship, and was successful. He then proposed to the Assembly that any person who had put to death a Roman citizen without allowing him to appeal to the people be considered a violator of the constitution. The proposal was carried. All knew that Cicero was meant, and he fled at once to Macedonia. His property was confiscated, his houses were destroyed, and his palace in the city was dedicated to the Goddess of Liberty,.

The kingdom of Cyprus, which had long been attached to that of Egypt, had been bequeathed to Rome at the death of Ptolemy Alexander in 80. The Senate had delayed to accept the bequest, and meanwhile the island was ruled by Ptolemy of Cyprus, one of the heirs of the dead king.

Clodius, on the plea that this king harboured pirates, persuaded the Assembly to annex the island, and to send Cato to take charge of it. He accepted the mission, and was absent two years. His duties were satisfactorily performed, and he returned with about $7,000,000 to increase the Roman treasury.

Thus Cicero and Cato being out of the city, the Senate was without a leader who could work injury in Caesar's absence.

CHAPTER 30

Caesar's Campaigns in Gaul

Caesar was now in the prime of manhood, in the full vigour of mind and body. His previous experience in camp life had been comparatively small. His early service in Asia, and his more recent campaigns in Spain, however, had shown his aptitude for military life.

The Romans had already obtained a foothold in Gaul. Since 118, the southern part of the country along the sea- board had been a Roman province, called **Gallia Narbonensis**, from the colony of Narbo which the Romans had founded. The rest of Gaul included all modern France, and a part of Switzerland, Holland, and Belgium. The inhabitants were all of the Celtic race, except a few Germans who had crossed the Rhine and settled in the North, and the **Aquitáni**, who lived in the Southwest and who are represented by the Basques of today.

The Gauls were more or less civilized since they had come into contact with the Romans, but they still had the tribal form of government, like the early Romans. There were more than fifty of these tribes, which were mostly hostile to one another, as well as divided into factions among themselves. This condition favoured a conquest, for the factions were frequently Roman and non-Roman. Two of the chief tribes were the **Aedui** and **Sequani**. The former had been taken under the protection of Rome; the latter, impatient of control and Roman influence, had invited a tribe of Germans under Ariovistus to come into Gaul and settle, and be their allies. These Germans had attacked and conquered the Aeduans, taken from them hostages, and with the Sequanians were in the ascendency.

In Switzerland lived the **Helvetii**. They had so increased in numbers that their country was too small for them. They therefore proposed to emigrate farther into Gaul, and the Sequanians, whose lands

116

bordered on those of the Helvetians, gave them permission to march through their country.

Such was the state of affairs when Caesar arrived in Gaul. Feeling that the passage of such a large body of. emigrants (368,000) through Gaul would be dangerous to the province (Gallia Narbonensis), he determined to interfere. The Helvetians were met at **Bibracte**, near Autun, and after a terrible battle, which raged from noon until night, were defeated with great slaughter (58). The survivors, about one third, were treated kindly, and most of them sent back to Switzerland.

Caesar now turned his attention to the Germans who had settled west of the Rhine. After several fruitless attempts at negotiation, during which the bad faith of Ariovistus became conspicuous, the forces came together. Though the Germans were brave, they were no match for the drilled legionaries, who fought with the regularity of a machine. Few of the barbarians escaped, but among these was Ariovistus.

The campaigns of this year being ended, the legions were sent into winter quarters among the Sequanians under Labiénus, the lieutenant of Caesar. He himself went into Cisalpine Gaul to attend to his duties as administrator, and to have communication with his friends at Rome.

The War with the Belgae.

While Caesar was in Hither Gaul, he learned from Labiénus that the **Belgae** were forming a league to resist the Romans. This people occupied the north-eastern part of Gaul, and embraced several tribes, of which the principal were the **Remi, Bellovaci, Suessiónes**, and **Nervii**. The last were the fiercest and least civilized.

Caesar raised two new legions, making eight in all, and marched against the Belgae as soon as the spring opened. His sudden approach alarmed the Remi, who lived nearest to Central Gaul, and they immediately put themselves under his protection. From them he learned that the Belgae could muster about 300,000 men.

By skilful tactics and a successful attack he put to flight and nearly annihilated the Suessiónes. The Bellovaci now put themselves under his protection, but the Nervii remained in arms. One day, while the six legions were forming camp on the bank of the River Sabis, the Nervii and their allies suddenly rushed upon them from an ambuscade in the woods on the opposite bank. The troops were entirely unprepared, and so quick was the enemy's charge that the Romans had not time to put on their helmets, to remove the covering from their shields, or to find their proper places in the ranks. Great confusion followed, and they became almost panic-stricken. Caesar rushed into their midst, snatched a shield from a soldier, and by his presence and coolness revived their courage. The Nervii were checked, and victory was assured. But the enemy fought on with a bravery that excited the admiration of Caesar. Of sixty thousand men scarcely five hundred survived. The women and children were cared for kindly by Caesar, and settled in their own territory.

The Aduatuci, who had assisted the Nervii in their struggle, were conquered by Caesar and sold into slavery.

Thus ended the Belgian campaign (57). The legions were put into winter quarters near where the war had been waged, and Caesar went to Italy. In his honour was decreed a thanksgiving lasting fifteen days.

THE VENETI.—INVASION OF GERMANY.

All the tribes in the north-western part of Gaul (Brittany) except the **Veneti** had given hostages to Crassus, son of the Triumvir, and lieutenant of Caesar. This tribe refused to give hostages, and, inducing others to join them, seized some Roman officers sent among them by Crassus. The campaign of the third year (56) was directed against these people. They were mostly sailors and fishermen, with villages built on the end of promontories and easily defended by land. In a naval engagement, which lasted nearly all day, their whole fleet was destroyed. The leaders of the Veneti were put to death for their treachery in seizing Roman officers, and the rest were sold into slavery.

The legions spent the winter of 56-55 in the northern part of Gaul, among the Aulerci and neighbouring tribes.

During this winter another wave of Germans passed over the Rhine into Gaul. They had been driven from their homes by a powerful tribe called the **Suevi**. In the spring of 55 Caesar collected his troops and advanced to within twelve miles of the German camp, and gave the invaders twenty-four hours to leave the country. Before the expiration of the time, they attacked Caesar's outposts, killing several Knights, and two men of aristocratic families. In the general engagement that followed, the Germans were totally routed and most of them were slain.

Caesar next determined to cross the Rhine into Germany, thinking thus to inspire the Germans with greater fear of the Romans. He built his famous bridge, crossed it, remained eighteen days in Germany, and, thinking his object accomplished, returned to Gaul, destroying the bridge behind him.

INVASION OF BRITAIN

It was now August and Caesar occupied the rest of the season by crossing the Channel to Britain (England). Landing near Deal, with but little resistance on the part of the natives, he explored the country for a short time, and returned in September, as the equinox was near and the weather unsettled. The legions were sent into winter quarters among the Belgae, and Caesar set out for Cisalpine Gaul.

During this winter (55-54), orders were given to build a large fleet, as Caesar intended to return to Britain the next year. After all preparations were completed, he set sail, July 20, 54, and the next day landed on the island. He defeated the Britons under their leader **Cassivelaunus**, and compelled them to pay tribute and give hostages. Many thousand prisoners were taken, and sold in Italy as slaves.

FINAL STRUGGLES OF THE GAULS.

In the winter of 54-53 the legions were distributed among several tribes. That stationed in the territory of the Eburónes was commanded by the lieutenants, Gabínus and Cotta. News reached the encampment that there was an uprisal of the Eburónes. It was decided to break up camp, and go, if possible, to the winter quarters of their nearest companions. On the march they were surprised and nearly all killed. Only a few stragglers carried the news to Labíenus, who was wintering with a legion among the Remi.

This success moved the Nervii to attack Quintus Cicero, the lieutenant who was wintering with his legion among them. Word was sent to Caesar, who had fortunately not yet left Gaul. He hastened to Cicero's relief, raised the siege, and all but annihilated the revolting Nervii.

In 53 Caesar punished the Eburónes for their action in the previous winter. The tribe was completely destroyed, but their leader, Ambiorix, escaped and was never captured. During this summer Caesar again crossed the Rhine. At the close of the summer he returned to Cisalpine Gaul, supposing that the Gauls were totally subdued. He was mistaken. The patriotism of the people was not yet extinguished. The chiefs of all the tribes secretly established communication with each other. A day was settled upon for a general uprising. The Roman inhabitants of Genabum, on the Liger, were massacred. The leading spirit in this last struggle of the Gauls was **Vercingetorix**, chief of the Averni.

Caesar hastened across the Alps, surmounted the difficulties of crossing the Cevennes when the snow was very deep, collected his legions, marched upon Genabum, and plundered and burnt the town.

Vercingetorix saw that he was no match for the legions in open battle. He proposed, therefore, to cut off Caesar's supplies by burning all the towns of the Bituriges, and laying the country waste. Avaricum alone was spared. Within its walls were placed the best of their goods and a strong garrison. Thither Caesar marched, and, after a well defended siege, captured the town and killed every person in it, excepting eight hundred, who escaped to the camp of Vercingetorix. Large quantities of corn were taken, with which Caesar supplied his soldiers. He then marched against Gergovia, the. capital of the Averni. As the town was on a high *plateau*, and too strong to be stormed, he laid siege to it.

A part of the army, contrary to instructions, one day attempted to assault the place. The battle which followed was disastrous to the Romans, and the only defeat Caesar received in Gaul. Forty-six officers and seven hundred men fell. The siege was raised. It was a serious position for Caesar. All Gaul was in flames. Retreating at once, he formed a junction with Labiénus at Agendicum, and with all his troops started for Gallia Narbonensis to protect it from invasion.

On his route was **Alesia**. Here Vercingetorix was intrenched with eighty thousand troops. It was, like Gergovia, situated on a hill and considered impregnable. Caesar laid siege to this place (52). Vercingetorix appealed to all Gaul for aid. Hardly had the fortress been invested when Caesar's army was surrounded by an immense force of Gauls that had come to the rescue. Caesar needed now all his skill and genius. But they did not fail him. The relieving army, though five times as large as his, was driven back and sent flying home.

Seeing that all was over, Vercingetorix called a council of his chiefs and advised surrender. A message was sent to Caesar. He demanded unconditional surrender, and was obeyed. The people were sold into slavery, and the money obtained distributed among the soldiers. Vercingetorix was kept to be exhibited in the triumph at Rome, and afterwards died in a dungeon.

With the fall of Alesia, the subjugation of Gaul was practically completed.

The next year (51) Caesar honoured several chiefs with privileges; some of the nobles were granted the franchise, and some admitted to the Senate. The work of Romanizing Gaul was fairly begun. Two provinces were formed, Gallia and Belgica, and later (17 *a. d.*) the former of these was subdivided into Lugdunensis and Aquitania. Roman money was introduced, and Latin became the official language.

CHAPTER 31

Clodius and Milo—Death of Crassus

During the nine years (59-50) passed by Caesar in Gaul, great confusion prevailed at Rome. The Republic needed a strong, firm hand, which would stop the shedding of blood and insure security of person and property. Pompey had attempted to bring about this result, but had failed. There were two prominent factions, one led by **Clodius**, the other by **Milo**.

> Clodius is the most extraordinary figure in this extraordinary period. He had no character. He had no distinguished talent save for speech; he had no policy; he was ready to adopt any cause or person which for the moment was convenient to him; and yet for five years this man was the leader of the Roman mob. He could defy justice, insult the Consuls, beat the Tribunes, parade the streets with a gang of armed slaves, killing persons disagreeable to him; and in the Senate itself he had high friends and connections, who threw a shield over him when his audacity had gone beyond endurance.

> Milo was as disreputable as Clodius. His chief fame had been gained in the schools of the gladiators. Gangs of armed slaves accompanied him everywhere, and there were constant collisions between his retainers and those of Clodius.

> In 57 Consuls were elected who favoured Cicero, and his recall was demanded. Clodius and his followers opposed the recall. The nobles, led by their tool Milo, pressed it Day after day the opposing parties met in bloody affrays. For seven months the brawl continued, till Milo's party finally got the ascendancy; the Assembly was convened, and the recall voted.

> For seventeen months Cicero had been in Greece, lamenting his

122

hard lot He landed at Brundisium on August 5, 57, and proceeded to Rome. Outside the city all men of note, except his avowed enemies, were waiting to receive him. The Senate voted to restore his property, and to rebuild his palace on the Palatine Hill and his other villas at the public expense. But Clodius, with his bands of ruffians, interrupted the workmen engaged in the repair of his Palatine house, broke down the walls, and, attacking Cicero himself, nearly murdered him.

At last Clodius even attempted to burn the house of Milo. The long struggle between these two ruffians culminated when Milo was a candidate for the consulship, and Clodius for the *praetorship*. The two meeting by accident in the Via Appia at Bovillae, Clodius was murdered, 20 January, 52. This act of violence strengthened Pompey, who was nominated sole Consul. Milo was impeached. His guilt was evident, and he went into exile at Massilia. Cicero prepared an elaborate speech in his defence, but did not dare to deliver it.

During the interval between the two campaigns of 57 and 56, Caesar renewed his alliance with his two colleagues in interviews that were held at Ravenna and Luca. He retained the command of Gaul; Pompey, that of Spain; Crassus, that of Syria.

Crassus now undertook the war against the Parthians. He was accompanied by his son, who had done good service under Caesar in Gaul. They arrived at Zeugma, a city of Syria, on the Euphrates; and the Romans, seven legions strong, with four thousand cavalry, drew themselves up along the river. The *Quaestor*, Cassius, a man of ability, proposed to Crassus a plan of the campaign, which consisted in following the river as far as Seleucia, in order not to be separated from his fleet and provisions, and to avoid being surrounded by the cavalry of the enemy. But Crassus allowed himself to be deceived by an Arab chief, who lured him to the sandy plains of Mesopotamia at Carrhae.

The forces of the Parthians, divided into many bodies, suddenly rushed upon the Roman ranks, and drove them back. The young Crassus attempted a charge at the head of fifteen hundred horsemen. The Parthians yielded, but only to draw him into an ambush, where he perished, after great deeds of valour. His head, carried on the end of a pike, was borne before the eyes of his unhappy father, who, crushed by grief and despair, gave the command into the hands of Cassius. Cassius gave orders for a general retreat The Parthians subjected the Roman army to continual losses, and Crassus himself was killed in a conference (53).

In this disastrous campaign there perished more than twenty thousand Romans. Ten thousand were taken prisoners and compelled to serve as slaves in the army of the Parthians.

The death of Crassus broke the Triumvirate; that of Julia, in 54, had sundered the family ties between Caesar and Pompey, who married Cornelia, the widow of the young Crassus, and daughter of Metellus Scipio.

CHAPTER 32

Caesar's Struggle with Pompey— Battle of Pharsalia

Pompey was elected sole Consul in February, 52. He at once threw off all pretence of an alliance with Caesar, and devoted himself to the interests of the Senate and aristocracy.

The brilliant successes of Caesar in Gaul had made a profound impression upon the minds of the citizens, to whom the name of the northern barbarians was still fraught with terror. Caesar had won for himself distinction as a soldier greater than the Scipios, or Sulla, or Pompey.

"He was coming back to lay at his country's feet a province larger than Spain, not only subdued, but reconciled to subjugation; a nation of warriors, as much devoted to him as his own legions."

The nobility had watched his successes with bitter envy; but they were forced to vote a thanksgiving of twenty days, which "the people made sixty."

Caesar now declared through his followers at Rome that he desired a second consulship. But he wished first to celebrate his triumph, and on this account would not disband his army; for, according to the custom, he could not triumph without it. According to another custom, however, he must disband it before he could offer himself as a candidate for the consulship. But he asked permission to set aside this custom, and to become a candidate while he was in the province in command of the army.

The law requiring a candidate to give up his command had been suspended several times before this; so that Caesar's request was reasonable. His enemies in the city were numerous and powerful, and he felt that, if he returned as a private citizen, his personal safety would be in danger; whereas, if he were a magistrate, his person would be considered sacred.

The Senate, on the other hand, felt that, if he carried his point, the days of their influence were numbered. Their first step, therefore, was to weaken Caesar, and to provide their champion, Pompey, with a force in Italy. They voted that Caesar should return to Pompey a legion which had been loaned him, and also should send another legion back to Italy. The vote was taken on the ostensible plea that the troops were needed in Asia Minor against the Parthians; but when they reached Italy they were placed under Pompey's command in Campania. The Consuls chosen for the year 49 were both bitter enemies of Caesar. He had taken up his winter quarters at Ravenna, the last town in his province bordering on Italy. From here he sent a messenger with letters to the Senate, stating that he was ready to resign his command, if Pompey did the same. The messenger arrived at Rome, January 1, 49, on the day in which the new Consuls entered upon their duties.

The letters were read in the Senate, and there followed a spirited discussion, resulting in a decree that Caesar should resign his command. The Tribunes opposed; but, being threatened by the Consuls, they were compelled to leave the city, and went directly to Ravenna.

When the action of the Senate was reported to Caesar, he called together his soldiers, and addressed them thus:

" For nine years I and my army have served our country loyally and with some degree of success. We have driven the Germans across the Rhine; we have made Gaul a province; and the Senate, for answer, has broken the constitution in setting aside the Tribunes who spoke in my defence. It has voted the state in danger, and has called Italy to arms, when no single act of mine can justify it in this course."

The soldiers became enthusiastic, and were eager to follow their leader without pay. Contributions were offered him by both men and officers. **Labiénus,** his trusted lieutenant, alone proved false. He stole away, and joined Pompey. Caesar then sent for two legions from across the Alps. With these legions he crossed the **Rubicon** into Italy, and marched to Ariminum.

Meanwhile the report of his movements reached Rome. The aristocracy had imagined that his courage would fail him, or that his army would desert. Thoroughly frightened, Consuls, *Praetors*, Senators,— leaving wives, children, and property to their fate,—fled from the city to seek safety with Pompey in Capua. They did not stop even to take the money from the treasury, but left it locked.

Caesar paused at Ariminum, and sent envoys to the Senate, stating that he was still desirous of peace. If Pompey would depart to his province in Spain, he would himself disband his own troops. He was even willing to have a personal interview with Pompey. This message was received by the Senate after its flight from Rome. The substance of its reply was, that Pompey did not wish a personal interview, but would go to Spain, and that Caesar must leave Ariminum, return to his province, and give security that he would dismiss his army.

These terms seemed to Caesar unfair, and he would not accept them. Accordingly he sent his lieutenant, Mark Antony, across the mountains to Arretium, on the road to Rome. He himself pushed on to Ancóna, before Pompey could stop him. The towns that were on his march threw open their gates, their garrisons joined his army, and their officers fled. Steadily he advanced, with constantly increasing forces, until when he reached Corfinium his army had swelled to thirty thousand troops.

This place had been occupied by Domitius with a party of aristocrats and a few thousand men. Caesar surrounded the town, and when Domitius endeavoured to steal away, his own troops took him and delivered him over to Caesar. The capture of Corfinium and the desertion of its garrison filled Pompey and his followers with dismay. They hurried to Brundisium, where ships were in readiness for them to depart.

Hoping to intercept Pompey, Caesar hastened to this port. On his arrival outside of the town, the Consuls, with half the army, had already gone. Pompey, however, was still within the place, with twelve thousand troops, waiting for transports to carry them away. He refused to see Caesar; and, though the latter endeavoured to blockade the port, he was unsuccessful, owing to want of ships.

Thus Pompey escaped. With him were the Consuls, more than half the Senate, and the aristocracy. Caesar would have followed them, but a fleet must first be obtained, and matters nearer home demanded his attention.

In sixty days Caesar had made himself master of Italy. On his way to Rome he met Cicero, and invited him to attend the Senate, but he preferred to stay away. Caesar entered the city unattended, and assembled the Senate through the Tribunes, Mark Antony and Cassius Longínus. The attendance was small, as most of the members were with Pompey. In his address to the Senate Caesar spoke of his own forbearance and concessions, of their unjust demands, and their violent suppression of the authority of the Tribunes. He was still willing to send envoys to treat with Pompey, but no one was found willing to go. After three days spent in useless discussion, Caesar decided to act for himself. By his own edict, he restored the children of the victims of Sulla's proscription to their rights and property. The money in the treasury was voted him by the Assembly of the people. He took as much of it as he needed, and started at once for Gaul to join his troops on his way to Spain.

He had much to accomplish. Spain was in the hands of Pompey's lieutenants, Afranius, Petreius, and Varro, who had six legions and allied troops. From Sicily and Sardinia came most of the grain supplies of Rome, and it was important to hold these islands. To Sicily he sent Curio and to Sardinia Valerius. Cato, who was in charge of Sicily, immediately abandoned it and fled to Africa. Sardinia received Caesar's troops with open arms.

Upon his arrival in Gaul, Caesar found that the inhabitants of Massilia had risen against his authority, led by the same Domitius whom he had sent away unharmed from Corfinium. Caesar blockaded the city, and, leaving Decimus Brutus in charge of operations, continued his journey to Spain. He found Afranius and Petreius strongly intrenched at **Ilerda** in Catalonia (Northern Spain). Within forty days he brought them to terms, and Varro, who was m Southern Spain, was eager to surrender. All Spain was at his feet.

Before leaving Spain, Caesar summoned the leading Spaniards and Romans to Cordova, for a conference. All promised obedience to his authority. He then set sail from Gades to Tarragóna, where he joined his legions and marched back to Massilia, which he found hard pressed and ready to surrender. The gates were opened. All were pardoned, and Domitius was allowed to escape a second time.

Caesar left a portion of his forces in Gaul, and with the rest arrived at Rome in the early winter of 49-48. Thus far he had been successful. Gaul, Spain, Sardinia, Sicily, and Italy were his. He had not succeeded, however, in getting together a naval force in the Adriatic, and he had lost his promising lieutenant, Curio, who had been surprised and killed in Africa, whither he had gone in pursuit of Cato and Pompey's followers.

During Caesar's absence, affairs at Rome had resumed their usual course. He had left the city under charge of his lieutenant, Aemilius Lepidus, and Italy in command of Mark Antony. Caesar was still at Massilia, when he learned that the people of Rome had proclaimed him Dictator. Financial troubles in the city had made this step necessary. Public credit was shaken. Debts had not been paid since the civil war began. Caesar allowed himself only eleven days in Rome. In this time estimates were drawn of all debts as they were one year before, the interest was remitted and the principal declared still due. This measure relieved the debtors somewhat.

It was now nearly a year since Caesar crossed the Rubicon. Pompey, during the nine months that had elapsed since his escape from Brundisium, had been collecting his forces in Epírus. Here had gathered many princes from the East, a majority of the Senatorial families of Rome, Cato and Cicero, the vanquished Afranius, and the renegade Labiénus. There were nine full legions, with cavalry and auxiliaries, amounting in all to 100,000 men.

Caesar reached Brundisium at the end of the year 49. His forces were fewer in number than those of his adversary, amounting to not more than 15,000 infantry and 600 cavalry. But his legionaries were all veterans, inured to toil and hunger, to heat and cold, and every man was devoted to his leader.

On the 4th of January he set sail from Brundisium, landing after an uneventful voyage at Acroceraunia. He advanced at once towards Dyrrachium where were Pompey's headquarters, occupied Apollonia, and intrenched himself on the left bank of the River Apsus. The country was well disposed and furnished him with ample supplies

Caesar sent back the vessels on which he crossed to transport his remaining troops, but they were intercepted on their way across and many of them destroyed. He was therefore compelled to confine himself to trifling operations, until his lieutenant, Mark Antony, could fit out a second fleet and bring over the remainder of his legions. When Antony finally crossed, he landed one hundred miles up the coast. Pompey's forces were between him and Caesar, and his position was full of danger; but Caesar marched rapidly round Dyrrachium, and joined him before Pompey knew of his movements.

The great general was now ready for action. He built a line of strongly fortified forts around Pompey's camp, blockading him by land. He turned the streams of water aside, causing as much inconvenience as possible to the enemy. So the siege dragged on into June.

Two deserters informed Pompey of a weak spot in Caesar's line. At this point Pompey made a sudden attack. For once Caesar's troops were surprised and panic-stricken. Even his own presence did not cause them to rally. Nearly one thousand of his men fell, thirty-two standards, and a few hundred soldiers were captured.

This victory was the ruin of Pompey's cause. Its importance was exaggerated. His followers were sure that the war was practically over; and so certain were they of ultimate success that they neglected to follow up the advantage gained, and gave Caesar opportunity to recover from the blow.

The latter now retired from the sea-board into Thessaly. Pompey followed, confident of victory. The nobles in his camp amused themselves with quarrelling about the expected spoils of war. Cato and Cicero remained behind in Epírus, the former disgusted at the actions of the degenerate nobility, the latter pleading ill health.

The two armies encamped on a plain in Thessaly near the River Enipeus, only four miles apart. Between them lay a low hill called Pharsálus, which gave name to the battle which followed.

The Battle of Pharsalia (August 9, 48) has acquired a special place in history, because it was fought by the Roman aristocracy in their own persons in defence of their own supremacy. Senators and the sons of Senators, the heirs of the names and fortunes of the ancient Roman families, the leaders of society in Roman salons, and the chiefs of the political party of the *optimates* (aristocracy) were here present on the field. The other great actions were fought by the ignoble multitude whose deaths were of less significance. The plains of Pharsalia were watered by the precious blood of the elect of the earth.

For several days the armies watched each other without decisive action. One morning towards the end of May (August 9, old style) Caesar noticed a movement in Pompey's lines that told him the expected attack was coming.

The position of the Senatorial army was well taken. Its right wing rested on the Enipeus, its left was spread out on the plain. Pompey himself commanded the left with the two legions the Senate had taken from Caesar. Outside him on the plain were his allies covered by the cavalry. Opposite Pompey was Caesar, with the famous Tenth Legion. His left and centre were led by his faithful Tribunes, Mark Antony and Cassius Longínus.

At the given signal Caesar's front ranks advanced on a run, threw their darts, drew their swords, and closed in. At once Pompey's cavalry charged, outflanking the enemy's right wing, and driving back the opposing cavalry, who were inferior in numbers. But as they advanced flushed with victory, Caesar's fourth line, which he had held in reserve, and which was made up of the flower of his legions, appeared in their way. So fierce was their attack that the Pompeians wavered, turned, and fled. They never rallied. The fourth line threw themselves upon Pompey's left wing, which was now unprotected. This wing, composed of Caesar's old veterans, was probably in no mood to fight its former comrades in arms. At any rate, it turned and fled. Pompey himself mounted his horse and rode off in despair. Thus the battle ended in a rout. But two hundred of Caesar's men fell, while fifteen thousand of the enemy lay dead on the field.

The abandoned camp was a remarkable sight The luxurious patricians had built houses of turf with ivy trained over the entrances to protect their delicate skins from the sun's rays; couches were stretched out ready for them to take repose after their expected victory, and tables were spread with dainty food and wines on which to feast. As he saw these preparations Caesar exclaimed, "These are the men who accused my suffering, patient army, which needed the common necessaries of life, of dissoluteness and profligacy." But Caesar could not delay. Leaving a portion of his forces in camp, by rapid marching he cut off the retreat of the enemy. Twenty-four thousand surrendered, all of whom were pardoned. Domitius, whom we saw at Corfinium and Massilia, was killed trying to escape. Labiénus, Afranius, and Petreius managed to steal away by night Thus ended the Battle of Pharsalia.

CHAPTER 33

Caesar's Operations in Egypt, Asia, Africa, and Spain

Pompey in his flight from Pharsalia, hastened by the shortest way to the sea, and, seeing a vessel weighing anchor, embarked with a few companions who had accompanied him in his flight. He went to Mityléne, and from there hoping to obtain an asylum with the young **Ptolemy**; but he was seized upon his arrival, and beheaded, 28 September, 48.

Just before his death Pompey had completed his fifty-eighth year.

Though he had some great and good qualities, he hardly deserved the surname of **Great**. He was certainly a good soldier, and is said to have excelled in all athletic sports, but he fell short of being a first-class general. He won great successes in Spain, and more especially in the East; but for these he was, no doubt, partly indebted to what others had already done. Of the gifts which make a good statesman, he had really none. He was too weak and irresolute to choose a side and stand by it Pitted against such a man as Caesar, he could not but fail. But to his credit be it said, that in a corrupt time he never used his opportunities for plunder and extortion.

Meanwhile Caesar, pursuing his victory with indefatigable activity, set sail for Egypt. Upon his arrival the head of his enemy was brought to him. He turned from the sight with tears in his eyes. The murderers now saw what would be their fate. Ptolemy was at variance with his sister, the famous **Cleopátra**. Caesar sided with her. The inhabitants of Alexandria revolted, and besieged Caesar in the palace; but with a handful of soldiers he bravely baffled their attacks. Setting fire to the neighbouring buildings, he escaped to his ships. Afterwards he returned and wreaked vengeance upon the Alexandrians, establishing Cleopátra upon the throne (47).

Satisfied with this vengeance, Caesar left Egypt, and went to Pontus, where **Pharnaces**, son of Mithradátes, was inciting a revolt against Rome. Caesar attacked and defeated him at **Zela** (47), with a rapidity rendered proverbial by his words, *Veni, vidi, vici,* **I came, I saw, I conquered**.

He now passed quickly down the Hellespont, and had landed in Italy before it was known that he had left Pontus. During his absence from the capital there had been some minor disturbances; but the mass of the citizens were firmly attached to him. Few could distrust the genius and fortune of the irresistible conqueror. In October of 48 he had been made Dictator a second time, and appointed Tribune for life.

Caesar's return in September, 47, was marked by no proscription. He insisted that all debts should be paid, and the rights of property respected. He restored quiet, and after a brief stay of three months prepared to transport his army to Africa. The army was in Campania, but discontented and mutinous because of not receiving the expected privilege of pillage and plunder. They refused to move until certain promised rewards were received. The Tenth Legion broke out into open revolt, and marched from Campania to Rome to obtain their rights. Caesar collected them in the Campus Martius, and asked them to state their grievances. They demanded their discharge. "I grant it, citizens" (*Quirites*), said the Imperator. Heretofore he had always addressed them as "fellow soldiers," and the implied rebuke was so keen, that a reaction at once began, and they all begged to be received again into his service. He accepted them, telling them that lands had been allotted to each soldier out of the *ager publicus*, or out of his own estates.

Africa must now be subdued. Since the defeat and death of Curio, King **Juba** had found no one to dispute his authority. Around him now rallied all the followers of Pompey, Metellus Scipio, Cato, Labiénus, Afranius, Petreius, and the slain general's two sons, Sextus and Gnaeus Pompeius.

Utica was made their headquarters. Here Cato collected thirteen legions of troops of miscellaneous character. Raids were made upon Sicily, Sardinia, and the coasts of Italy. Caesar's officers, if captured, were put to death without mercy.

Cicero alone of the old Pompeian party protested against such cruelties. He remained in Italy, was denounced by them as a traitor, and charged with currying favour of the Dictator.

Caesar sailed from Lilybaeum (December 19), effected a landing near Leptis, and maintained himself in a fortified position until he formed useful alliances among the Mauretanians. Many Roman residents in the province came to him, indignant at Metellus Scipio's promise to Juba to give the province to him in case of success. Many deserters also came in, enraged that precedence was given to Juba over Scipio in councils of war. But the enemy's army was kept full of new recruits sent from Utica by Cato.

For three months Caesar failed to bring on the desired engagement; Scipio had learned caution from Pompey's experience at Pharsalia. Finally, at Thapsus, one hundred miles southeast of Carthage, April 4, 46, the armies met. Caesar's men were so enthusiastic that they rushed to the charge with one impulse. There was no real battle, but rather a slaughter. Officers and men fled for their lives. Scipio was intercepted in his flight and slain. Juba and Petreius fled together, but, finding their retreat cut off, engaged, it is said, in mortal combat; when the first, Petreius, fell, the other threw himself on his own sword. Labiénus and the two sons of Pompey managed to escape to Spain. Afranius was captured and executed.

Cato, when he heard of the defeat, retired to his chamber in Utica, and committed suicide.

Thus ended the African campaign.

On his return from. Africa, Caesar celebrated four triumphs, on four successive days; one over the Gauls, one over Ptolemy of Egypt, one over Pharnaces, and one over Juba. He gratified his armed followers with liberal gifts, and pleased the people by his great munificence. They were feasted at a splendid banquet, at which were twenty- two thousand tables, each table having three couches, and each couch three persons. Then followed shows in the circus and theatre, combats of wild beasts and gladiators, in which the public especially delighted.

Honours were now heaped upon Caesar without stint. A thanksgiving of forty days was decreed. His statue was placed in the Capitol. Another was inscribed to Caesar the Demigod. A golden chair was allotted to him in the Senate-House. The name of the fifth month (*Quintilis*) of the Roman calendar was changed to **Julius** (July). He was appointed Dictator for two years, and later for life. He received for three years the office of Censor, which enabled him to appoint Senators, and to be guardian of manners and morals. He had already been made Tribune (48) for life, and Pontifex Maximus (63). In a word, he was king in everything excepting name.

Caesar's most remarkable and durable reform at this period was the **Revision** of the **Calendar**. The Roman method of reckoning time had been so inaccurate, that now their seasons were more than two months behind. Caesar established a calendar, which, with slight changes, is still in use. It went into operation January 1st, 45. He employed Sosigenes, an Alexandrian astronomer, to superintend the reform.

While Sosigenes was at work on the calendar, Caesar purified the Senate. Many who were guilty of extortion and corruption were expelled, and the vacancies filled with persons of merit.

Meanwhile matters in Spain were not satisfactory. After the battle of Pharsalia, Cassius Longínus, Trebonius, and Marcus Aemilius Lepidus had been sent to govern the province. They could not agree. The soldiers became mutinous. To Spain flocked all who were dissatisfied with Roman affairs. The remnant of Scipio's African army rested there in its wanderings. Thus Labiénus and Pompey's two sons managed to collect an army as numerous as that which had been defeated at Thapsus. There were thirteen legions in all.

Caesar saw that he must make one more struggle. He set out for the province accompanied by his nephew **Octavius** (afterwards the Emperor **Augustus**), and by his trusted friend and officer, **Decimus Brutus**. The struggle in Spain was protracted for several months, but the decisive battle was fought at **Munda**, 17 March, 45, on the Guadalquivir, near Cordova. The forces were well matched. The advantage in position was on the side of the enemy. The battle was stubbornly fought, most of it hand to hand, with short swords. So equal was the struggle, so doubtful at one time the issue, that Caesar himself sprang from his horse, seized a standard, and rallied a wavering legion. Finally, Labiénus was seen to gallop across the field. It was thought he was fleeing. Panic seized his troops, they broke and ran. Thirty thousand were slain, including three thousand Roman Knights, and Labiéus himself.

Gnaeus Pompey shortly after lost his life, but Sextus for a number of years.

Caesar tarried in Spain, regulating affairs, until late in autumn, when he returned to Rome and enjoyed another triumph over the Iberians (Spaniards). The triumph was followed, as usual, by games and festivals, which kept the populace in a fever of delight and admiration.

Cato.—Metellus Scipio.

Marcus Portius Cato Uticensis[1] (95-46) was the great-grandson of Cato the Censor. He was the last of the Romans of the old school. Like his more famous ancestor, he was frugal and austere in his habits, upright, unselfish, and incorruptible. But he was a fanatic, who could not be persuaded to relinquish his views on any subject. As a general, he was a failure, having neither taste nor genius for military exploits. He held various offices at Rome, as *Quaestor* and *Praetor*, but when candidate for the consulship he was defeated, because he declined to win votes by bribery and other questionable methods then in vogue.

Quintus Caecilius Metellus Pius belonged to the illustrious family of the Scipios by birth, and to that of the Metelli by adoption. He was one of the most unjust and dishonest of the Senators that opposed Caesar. He was the father-in-law of Pompey, by whom he was made a pliant tool against the great conqueror.

---

1. Cato the Younger, called **Uticensis** on account of his death at Utica.

CHAPTER 34

Murder of Caesar

Upon his return from Spain, Caesar granted pardon to all who had fought against him, the most prominent of whom were **Gaius Cassius**, **Marcus** Brutus, and **Cicero**. He increased the number of the Senate to nine hundred. He cut off the corn grants, which nursed the city mob in idleness. He sent out impoverished men to colonize old cities. He rebuilt Corinth, and settled eighty thousand Italians on the site of Carthage. As a censor of morals he was very rigid. His own habits were marked by frugality. The rich young patricians were forbidden to be carried about in litters, as had been the custom. Libraries were formed. Eminent physicians and scientists were encouraged to settle in Rome. The harbour of Ostia was improved, and a road constructed from the Adriatic to the Tyrrhenian Sea, over the Apennines. A temple to Mars was built, and an immense amphitheatre was erected at the foot of the Tarpeian Rock.

In the midst of this useful activity he was basely murdered.

Cassius Longínus and **Marcus Junius Brutus** were the leaders in the conspiracy to effect Caesar's death. Cassius, a former lieutenant of Crassus, had shown great bravery in the war with the Parthians. At Pharsalia he fought on the side of Pompey, but was afterwards pardoned by Caesar. He was married to a sister of Brutus. The latter, a nephew and son-in-law of Cato, had also fought at Pharsalia against Caesar, and also been pardoned by him. Cassius, it was said, hated the tyrant, and Brutus tyranny.

These conspirators were soon joined by persons of all parties; and men who had fought against each other in the civil war now joined hands. Cicero was not taken into the plot. He was of advanced years, and all who knew him must have felt that he would never consent to the taking the life of one who had been so lenient towards his conquered enemies.

On the morning of the **Ides** (15th) of March, 44, as Caesar entered the Senate and took his seat, he was approached by the conspirators, headed by Tullius Cimber, who prayed for the pardon of his exiled brother; and while the rest joined him in the request, he, grasping Caesar's hand, kissed his head and breast. As Caesar attempted to rise, Cimber dragged his cloak from his shoulders, and Casca, who was standing behind his chair, stabbed him in the neck. The first blow was struck, and the whole pack fell upon their noble victim. Cassius stabbed him in the face, and Marcus Brutus in the groin. He made no further resistance; but, wrapping his gown over his head and the lower part of his body, he fell at the base of **Pompey's Statue**, which was drenched with the martyr's blood.

Great tumult and commotion followed; and, in their alarm most of the Senators fled. It was two days before the Senate met, the conspirators meanwhile having taken refuge in the Capitol. Public sentiment was against them. Many of Caesar's old soldiers were in the city, and many more were flocking there from all directions. The funeral oration of Mark Antony over the remains produced a deep impression upon the crowd. They became so excited when the speaker removed the dead man's toga, and disclosed his wounds, that, instead of allowing the body to be carried to the Campus Martius for burial, they raised a funeral pile in the Forum, and there burned it. The crowd then dispersed in troops, broke into and destroyed the houses of the conspirators. Brutus and Cassius fled from the city for their lives, followed by the other murderers.

As a general Caesar was probably superior to all others, excepting possibly Hannibal. He was especially remarkable for the fertility of his resources. It has been said that Napoleon taught his enemies how to conquer him; but Caesar's enemies never learned how to conquer him, because he had not a mere system of tactics, but a new stratagem for every emergency. He was, however, not only a great general, but a pre-eminent statesman, and second only to Cicero in eloquence. As a historian, he wrote in a style that was clear, vigorous, and also simple. Most of his writings are lost; but of those that remain Cicero said that fools might try to improve on them, but no wise man would attempt it.

CHAPTER 35

The Second Triumvirate—Philippi and Actium

Caesar in his will had appointed **Gaius Octavius**, the grandson of his sister Julia, heir to three fourths of his property; and his other relatives were to have the remaining fourth.

Young Octavius was in his nineteenth year when Caesar was murdered. He went at once to Rome to claim his inheritance. Caesar's widow, Calpurnia, had intrusted to Mark Antony all the money in the house,—a large sum,—and had also delivered to his care all the Dictator's writings and memoranda.

Octavius was cool and sagacious, without passion or affection, and showed himself a match for all his opponents. His arrival at Rome was disagreeable to Antony, who was unwilling to surrender Caesar's property. He claimed that he had already expended it for public purposes. Octavius at once paid the dead Dictator's legacies, mostly out of his own fortune, thus making himself very popular among the people. He then joined the party of the Senate, and during the autumn and winter of 44 was its chief champion. He was helped by the eloquent Cicero, who was delivering against Antony his famous fourteen **Philippics**,—so called from their resemblance to the great orations of Demosthenes against Philip.

During the spring of 43 Octavius advanced against Antony, who was at Mutina (Modena), and defeated him in two battles. He was then appointed Consul, and, finding it for his interest, he deserted the Senate, made friends with Antony, and with him and Lepidus formed (27 November, 43) the **Second Triumvirate**, assuming full authority to govern and reorganize the state, and to hold office for five years.

The provinces were divided as follows: Lepidus was to have Spain and Gallia Narbonensis; Antony, the rest of Gaul beyond the Alps and Gallia Cisalpina; Octavius, Sicily, Sardinia, and Africa. A bloody prescription followed. Among its victims were **Cicero**, who was surrendered to please Antony, 300 Senators, and 2,000 *Equites*.

PHILIPPI AND ACTIUM.

The Triumvirs could now concentrate their energies upon the East, whither **Brutus** and **Cassius**, the murderers of Caesar, had fled. These two had organized in the provinces of the East an army amounting to 80,000 infantry and 20,000 cavalry. They were employed in plundering various towns of Asia Minor, and finally, in the spring of 42, assembled their forces at Sardis preparatory to an invasion of Europe. After marching through Thrace they entered Macedonia, and found Antony and Octavius opposed to them at **Philippi**, with an army of 120,000 troops.

There were two battles at Philippi in November, 42. In the first, Brutus defeated Octavius; but Cassius was defeated by Antony, and, unaware of his colleague's victory, committed suicide. In the second battle, three weeks later, Brutus was defeated by the united armies of the Triumvirs, and, following the example of Cassius, put an end to his life. With Brutus fell the Republic. The absolute ascendency of individuals, which is monarchy, was then established.

The immediate result of Philippi was a fresh arrangement of the Roman world among the Triumvirs. Antony preferred the East, Octavius took Italy and Spain, and Africa fell to Lepidus.

Octavius tried to establish order in Italy, but many obstacles were to be overcome. Sextus Pompeius, who had escaped from Munda, was in command of a strong naval force. He controlled a large part of the Mediterranean, and, by waylaying the corn ships bound for Rome, exposed the city to great danger from famine. Octavius was obliged to raise a fleet and meet this danger. At first he was defeated by Pompey, but later, in 36, in the great sea-fight off **Naulochus** in Sicily, the rebel was overcome. He fled to Asia with a few followers, but was taken prisoner at Milétus by one of the lieutenants of Antony, and put to death.

Lepidus now claimed Sicily as a part of his province, and an equal share in the government of the Roman world with the other Triumvirs. But his soldiers were induced to desert him, and he was obliged to surrender to Octavius. His life was spared, but he was deprived of his power and provinces. He lived twenty years longer (until 13), but ceased to be a factor in public affairs. Having rid themselves of all rivals, Octavius and Antony redivided the Empire, the former taking the West, the latter the East.

Antony now repaired to Alexandria, and surrendered himself to the fascinations of the famous Cleopátra, He assumed the habits and dress of an Eastern monarch, and by his senseless follies disgusted his friends and supporters. He resigned himself to luxury and idleness, and finally divorced himself from his wife **Octavia**, sister of Octavius, disregarding his good name and the wishes of his friends. Thus gradually he became more and more estranged from Octavius, until finally the rupture resulted in open war.

The contest was decided by the naval battle off Cape **Actium**, in Greece, September 2, 31. Antony had collected from all parts of the East a large army, in addition to his fleet, which was supported by that of Cleopátra. He wished to decide the contest on land; but Cleopátra insisted that they should fight by sea. The fleet of Octavius was commanded by **Agrippa**, who had been in command at the sea-fight off Naulochus. The battle lasted a long time, and was still undecided, when Cleopátra hoisted sail and with her sixty vessels hastened to leave the line. Antony at once followed her. The battle, however, continued until his remaining fleet was destroyed, and his army, after a few days' hesitation, surrendered.

Octavius did not follow Antony for about a year. He passed the winter in Samos, sending Agrippa to Italy with the veterans. His time was occupied in restoring order in Greece and Asia, in raising money to satisfy the demands of his troops, and in founding new colonies. At length he turned his attention to Egypt. After capturing Pelusium, the key of the country, he marched upon Alexandría. Antony, despairing of success, committed suicide, expiring in the arms of Cleopátra. The queen, disdaining to adorn the triumph of the conqueror, followed his example, and was found dead on her couch, in royal attire, with her two faithful attendants also dead at her feet.

Octavius was now sole ruler of Rome. Before returning to the capital to celebrate his triumphs, he organized Egypt as a province, settled disputes in Judaea, and arranged matters in Syria and Asia Minor. He arrived at Rome (August 29), and enjoyed three magnificent triumphs. The gates of the temple of **Janus**—which were open in time of war, and had been closed but twice before, once during Numa's reign, and once between the First and Second Punic Wars—were closed, and Rome was at peace with all the world.

MARCUS TULLIUS CICERO.

Cicero's public life covered a period of nearly forty years, from the dictatorship of Sulla to the fall of the Republic. Although endowed by nature with great talents, he was always under the sway of the moment, and therefore little qualified to be a statesman; yet he had not sufficient self-knowledge to see it. Hence the attempts he made to, play a part in politics served only to lay bare his utter weakness. Thus it happened that he was used and then pushed aside, attracted and repelled, deceived by the weakness of his friends and the" strength of his adversaries; and at last threatened by both the parties between which he tried to steer his course.

CHAPTER 36

Augustus (30 b. c—14 a. d.)

After enjoying his triple triumph, Octavius should, according to the precedents of the Republic, have given up the title of **Imperator**; but he allowed the Senate, which was only too glad to flatter him, to give him that name for ten years,—a period which was repeatedly renewed. In this way he became permanent commander of the national forces. Next the Imperator (Emperor) caused himself to be invested with the authority of Censor. This enabled him to revise the list of Senators, and to restore to this body something of its ancient respectability. By judicious pruning he reduced the number to six hundred, and required a property qualification for membership. He placed himself at its head as **Princeps** (prince), a title which implied that the Emperor was the *first* citizen, without claiming any rights of royalty, thus lulling any suspicions of the populace.

The Senate still decided the most important questions. It had jurisdiction in criminal matters, and the right of ratifying new laws. It was convened three times each month; *viz.* on the 1st, 5th (or 7th), and 13th (or 15th). The Emperor voted with the other Senators.

The Senate next conferred upon Octavius the title of **Augustus**; then it made him Proconsul (an officer with the right to govern provinces), and Consul, with the privilege of having twelve *lictors*, and of sitting in the *curule* chair between the two Consuls. The regular Consuls, of course, were only too ready to follow his wishes. Finally, he was made Pontifex Maximus, the head of the Roman religion.

Augustus was now supreme ruler in fact, if not in name. The Senate was practically subject to his will. The Assemblies gradually lost all voice in the government, and finally disappeared entirely. The Senate, however, continued nominally to act until the time of Diocletian (284 *a.d.*).

As Augustus had exclusive command of the armies, he chose to govern as Proconsul those provinces which required military forces. He himself resided at the capital, and sent deputies (*legati*) to oversee them. The other provinces, called Senatorial, were governed by Proconsuls appointed by the Senate. These were at this time Sicily, Africa, Achaia (Greece), Macedonia, Asia (Minor), Hispania Ulterior, and Gallia Narbonensis.

The city government now included all Italy. In this Augustus was assisted by three *Praefects*; one in charge of the corn supplies, a second in charge of the city proper, and a third in charge of his bodyguard of nine thousand men, called the **Praetorian Guard**. These *Praefects* soon overshadowed all the regular magistrates, and through them Augustus reigned supreme.

The Roman Empire at this time included all the countries bordering on the Mediterranean, extending east to the Parthian kingdom (the Upper Euphrátes) and the Arabian Desert, south to the Desert of Sahára, and west to the Atlantic Ocean. On the north the boundary was unsettled, and subject to inroads of barbarians. In the early part of his reign Augustus joined to the Empire a new province, **Moesia**, comprising the territory along the Lower Danube, and making nineteen in all.

Augustus next devoted himself to the task of conquering the territory between the Lower Rhine and Moesia, which was occupied by hardy mountaineers whose resistance was likely to be stubborn. His two stepsons, **Drusus** and **Tiberius**, were in charge of this important work. They were so successful as to acquire enough territory to form two new provinces, **Rhaetia** and **Noricum** (15 B. c).

Tiberius also conquered the valley of the Save, and made it the province of **Pannonia** (Western Hungary), 10 b. c.

Drusus, while his brother Tiberius was engaged in Pannonia, made a campaign against the Germans near the Rhine. He had nearly finished the conquest of Germany from the Rhine to the Elbe, when he died (9 b. c), and was succeeded by his brother Tiberius, who completed his work.

Drusus received the cognomen of **Germanicus** for his conquests in Germany. His wife was Antonia, daughter of Mark Antony, by whom he had two sons, Germanicus and Claudius, the latter of whom was afterwards Emperor.

In 7 *A. D.* **Lucius Varus** was appointed governor of the newly acquired territory in Germany. When he endeavoured to subject these recently conquered peoples to the forms of the Roman provincial government, they rose in rebellion under the lead of **Arminius** (Herman), a powerful chief.

Varus was allured from his fortified camp (9 *a. d.*) into a pass in the **Teutoberger Forests**, where he was suddenly attacked on all sides. After three days' fighting, he succeeded with great loss in making his way through the pass into the open plain, but was there met by the enemy in full force, and his troops were annihilated. In despair Varus killed himself. Germany was practically lost and the Rhine became again the Roman frontier. This defeat caused a great stir at Rome, and the Emperor is said to have exclaimed in his sorrow, "Varus, Varus, give me back my legions!"

Five years later (14 *a. d.*) Augustus died. In his last moments he asked his friends if he had not played well his part in the comedy of life.

Although married three times, the Emperor had but one child, **Julia** (39 b. c.—14 *a. d.*), by his second wife, Scribonia. She was noted for her beauty and talents, but infamous for her intrigues. She was married three times; first, to Marcellus, her cousin; secondly, to Agrippa, by whom she had five children; and thirdly, to the Emperor Tiberius. She was banished on account of her conduct, and died in want.

Octavia, the sister of Augustus, was noted for her beauty and accomplishments, as well as for the nobility of her character. Her son **Marcellus** was adopted by his uncle, but died young (23 b. c). The famous lines of Virgil upon this promising young man (Aeneid VI. 869-887) were read before the Emperor and his sister, moving them to tears, and winning for the author a munificent reward.

After the death of her first husband, Octavia was married to Mark Antony, by whom she had two daughters, through whom she was the ancestress of three Emperors, **Claudius**, **Caligula**, and **Nero**.

Agrippa (63-12), an eminent general and statesman, was a warm friend and counsellor of Augustus. At the Battle of Actium he commanded the fleet of Octavius. He married Julia, the only daughter of the Emperor, and had three sons, two of whom were adopted by Augustus, but died before him; the third was murdered by Tiberius.

Augustus died at the age of seventy-six. He was frugal and correct in his personal habits, quick and shrewd in his dealings with men, bold and ambitious in the affairs of state. His greatness consisted rather in the ability to abstain from abusing the advantages presented by fortune, than in the genius which moulds the current of affairs to the will. His success depended on the temper of the people and the peculiar circumstances of the time. His clearest title to greatness is found in the fact that he compelled eighty millions of people to live in peace for more than forty years. He made the world to centre on one will, and the horrors which mark the reigns of his successors were the legitimate result of the irresponsible sovereignty he established. He formed his empire for the present, to the utter ignoring of the future. Thus it would seem that the part he played was that of a shrewd politician, rather than that of a wise statesman.

CHAPTER 37

The Augustan Age

In speaking of Augustus, we must take into account the writers whose names have given to his its brightest lustre, and have made the **Augustan Age** a synonym for excellence in culture, art, and government. Virgil, Ovid, Horace, Livy, and a host of others, have given his reign a brilliancy unmatched in time, which is rather enhanced than diminished by the fame of Cicero, Caesar, and Sallust, who produced that of Tacitus, Seneca, and others, who followed; for they belong to an epoch in which Augustus stands the central figure in all which pertains to the arts of peace.

In literature the name of **Virgil** stands first in the Augustan age. Born at Andes, near Mantua, 15 October, 70, he was educated at Cremóna and Mediolánum. After completing his education he retired to his paternal estate. In the division of land among the soldiers after the Battle of Philippi (42), he was deprived of his property, which was subsequently restored to him by Augustus. He lived partly at Rome, partly in Campania. His health was never good, and he died in his fifty-second year (22 September, 19 b. c).

Virgil had neither original nor creative genius. Though he mainly imitated Greek poetry, his style is graceful and eloquent, his tone inspiring and elevating.

In disposition he was childlike, innocent, and amiable,—a good son, a faithful friend, honest, and full of devotion to persons and ideal interests. He was not, however, fitted to grapple with the tasks and difficulties of practical life.

In his fortunes and friends he was a happy man. Munificent patronage gave him ample means of enjoyment and leisure; and he had the friendship of all the most accomplished men of his day, among whom was Horace, who entertained a strong affection for him. His

147

fame, which was established in his lifetime, was cherished after his death as an inheritance in which every Roman had a share; and his works became schoolbooks even before the death of Augustus, and have continued such ever since.

Horace (65-8 b. c.) was born at Venusia, but received his education at Rome and Athens. He was present at the Battle of Philippi (42), where he fought as Tribune under Brutus. His first writings were his *Satires*. These he read to his friends, and their merit was at once recognized. His great patron was **Maecénas**, who introduced him to the Emperor, and gave him a fine country seat near Tivoli, among the Sabine Mountains. He died the same year as his patron, and was buried beside him at the Esquiline Gate.

The poems of Horace give us a picture of refined and educated life in the Rome of his time. They are unsurpassed in gracefulness and felicity of thought. Filled with truisms, they were for centuries read and quoted more than those of any other ancient writer.

Ovid (43 B.C.—18 *a. d.*), a native of Sulmo, is far inferior to Virgil and Horace as a poet, but ranks high on account of his great gift for narration.

"Of the Latin poets he stands perhaps nearest to modern civilization, partly on account of his fresh and vivid sense of the beauties of nature, and partly because his subject is love. His representations of this passion are graceful, and strikingly true. He also excelled other poets in the perfect elegance of his form, especially in the character and rhythm of his verses."

He spent his last days in exile, banished by Augustus for some reason now unknown. Some of his most pleasing verses were written during this period.

One of the most noted men of the Augustan age was **Maecénas**, the warm friend and adviser of Augustus. He was a constant patron of the literature and art of his generation. He was very wealthy, and his magnificent house was the centre of literary society in Rome. He helped both Virgil and Horace in a substantial manner, and the latter is constantly referring to him in his poetry. He died (8 b. c.) childless, and left his fortune to Augustus.

The prose writers who lived at this period were Livy, Sallust, and Nepos.

Livy is the best of these. He was a native of Patavium (Padua), a man of rhetorical training, who spent most of his time in Rome. The historical value of his work cannot be overestimated, on account of the scarcity, and in many cases the utter lack, of other historical documents on the times of which he wrote. His style is spirited, and always interesting. His accuracy, however, is not to be compared with that of Caesar. Only thirty-five out of the one hundred and forty-two books that he wrote are preserved.

Nepos was a prolific writer, but only a portion of one of his works, *De Viris Illustribus*, has come down to us; it is neither accurate nor interesting, and of little value.

Sallust left two historical productions, one on the conspiracy of Catiline, the other on the war with Jugurtha. His style is rhetorical. He excels in delineating character, but he is often so concise as to be obscure.

Gaius Asinius Pollio was a statesman and orator of marked attainments of this time. He was strongly attached to the old republican institutions, a man of great independence of character, and a poet of no mean merit, as his contemporaries testify. Unfortunately, none of his writings are preserved.

The age of Augustus is also noted for the architectural improvements in Rome. Augustus is said to have found a city of stone, and left one of marble. He himself built twelve temples, and repaired eighty-two that had fallen into decay. The **Forum** was beautified by five halls of justice (*Basilicae*), which were erected around its borders. The most famous of these was the **Basilica Julia**, begun by Julius Caesar and finished by Augustus. Public squares were planned and begun north of the great Forum, the finest of which was the **Forum of Trajan**, finished by the Emperor of that name.

The finest building outside of the city, in the Campus Martius, was the **Pantheon**, built by Agrippa, and now used as a Christian church. Here are buried many distinguished men. Nearby, Augustus erected a mausoleum for himself. Here too was a theatre, built by Pompey,—the first stone theatre of Rome.

CHAPTER 38

The Julian and Claudian Emperors
Tiberius (14-37 a. d.)

Augustus was succeeded by **Tiberius Claudius Nero Caesar** (born 42 b. c), the son of Tiberius Claudius Nero and Livia. His mother obtained a divorce from Tiberius, and married Augustus.

Tiberius had great military talent. He was a severe disciplinarian, and commanded the full confidence of his soldiers. As commander in Cantabria, Armenia, Rhaetia, Dalmatia, and Germany, he conducted his campaigns with success, and honour to himself. Returning to Rome in 7 b. c, he celebrated a triumph, and afterwards married Julia, the dissolute daughter of Augustus. This marriage proved to be the ruin of Tiberius, developing everything that was bad in his character, and making him jealous, suspicious, and hypocritical.

Augustus, not relishing the changes in his character, sent him to Rhodes, where he lived seven years in retirement. Through his mother's influence, however, he was recalled in 2 *a.d.*, and was afterwards appointed the Emperor's successor.

He ascended the throne at the age of fifty-six. A silent man, "all his feelings, desires, and ambitions were locked behind an impenetrable barrier." He is said but once to have taken counsel with his officers. He was a master of dissimulation, and on this account an object of dislike and suspicion. But until his later years, his intellect was clear and far-seeing, penetrating all disguises.

Throughout his reign Tiberius strove to do his duty to the Empire at large, and maintained with great care the constitutional forms which had been established by Augustus. Only two changes of importance were made. First, the **Imperial Guard**, hitherto seen in the city only in small bodies, was permanently encamped in full force close to the walls. By this course the danger of riots was much lessened. Secondly, the old **Comitias** were practically abolished. But the Senate was treated with great deference.

Tiberius expended great care on the provinces. His favourite maxim was, that a good shepherd should shear, and not flay, his sheep. Soldiers, governors, and officials of all kinds were kept in a wholesome dread of punishment, if they oppressed those under them. Strict economy in public expenses kept the taxes down. Commerce was cherished, and his reign on the whole was one of prosperity for the Empire.

Tiberius was noted especially for prosecutions for **Majestas**, on the slightest pretext. *Majestas* nearly corresponds to treason; but it is more comprehensive. One of the offences included in the word was effecting, aiding in, or planning the death of a magistrate, or of one who had the *imperium* or *potestas*. Tiberius stretched the application of this offence even to words or conduct which could in any way be considered dangerous to the Emperor. A hateful class of informers (*delatores*) sprung up, and the lives of all were rendered unsafe. The dark side of this ruler's character is made specially prominent by ancient historians; but their statements are beginning to be taken with much allowance.

After a reign of twenty-three years, Tiberius died, either in a fainting fit or from violence, at the age of seventy-nine.

Livia, the mother of Tiberius, deserves more than a passing notice. She exercised almost a boundless influence on her husband, Augustus. She had great ambition, and was very cruel and unscrupulous. She managed to ruin, one after another, the large circle of relatives of Augustus, until finally the aged Emperor found himself alone in the palace with Livia and her son, Tiberius. All Rome execrated the Empress, and her son feared and hated her. She survived Augustus fifteen years, and died in 29. Tiberius refused to visit her on her death-bed, and was not present at her funeral

Sejánus was the commander of the Praetorian Guard of Tiberius. He was trusted fully by the Emperor, but proved to be a deep-dyed rascal. He persuaded Livilla, the daughter-in-law of the Emperor, to poison her husband, the heir apparent, and then he divorced his own wife to marry her. He so maligned Agrippína, the widow of Germanicus and daughter of Agrippa and Julia, that Tiberius banished her, with her sons Nero and Drusus. In 26 he induced the Emperor to retire to the island of Capreae, and he himself became the real master of Rome.

Tiberius at last finding out his true character, Sejánus was arrested and executed in 31. His body was dragged through the streets, torn in pieces by the mob, and thrown into the Tiber.

CALIGULA (37–41).

Tiberius having left no son, the Senate recognized Gaius Caesar, son of Germanicus and Agrippína, grandson of Julia, and great-grand-son of Augustus, as Emperor. He is better known as **Caligula**,—a nickname given him by the soldiers from the buskins he wore. He was twenty-five years of age when he began to reign, of weak constitution, and subject to fits. After squandering his own wealth, he killed rich citizens, and confiscated their property. He seemed to revel in blood-shed, and is said to have expressed a wish that the Roman people had but one neck, that he might slay them all at a blow. He was passion-ately fond of adulation, and often repaired to the Capitoline temple in the guise of a god, and demanded worship. Four years of such a tyrant was enough. He was murdered by a Tribune of his Praetorian Guard.

THE CLAUDIAN EMPERORS
CLAUDIUS (41–54).

A strong party was now in favour of returning to a republican form of government; but while the Senate was considering this question, the Praetorian Guard settled it by proclaiming **Claudius** Emperor.

Claudius was the uncle of Caligula and the nephew of Tiberius. He was a man of learning and good parts, but a glutton, and the slave of his two wives, who were both bad women. His first wife, **Messalí-na**, was so notorious that her name has became almost a synonym for wickedness. His second wife, his niece **Agrippína**, sister of Caligula, was nearly as bad. This woman had by her former husband, Domitius, a son, whom she induced the Emperor to adopt under the name of **Nero**. The faithless wife then caused her husband to be poisoned, and her son to be proclaimed Emperor.

At Rome the rule of Claudius was mild, and on the whole ben-eficial. In the government of the provinces he was rigorous and se-vere. He undertook the **Conquest of Britain**, and in a campaign of sixteen days he laid the foundation of its final subjugation, which occurred about forty years later, under the noted general **Agricola**. It remained a Roman province for four hundred years, but the peo-ple never assimilated Roman customs, as did the Gauls, and when the Roman garrisons were withdrawn, they quickly returned to their former condition. However, many remains of Roman buildings in the island show that it was for the time well under subjection.

The public works of Claudius were on a grand scale. He constructed a new harbour at the mouth of the Tiber, and built the great aqueduct called the **Aqua Claudia**, the ruined arches of which can be seen to this day. He also reclaimed for agriculture a large tract of land by draining the Fucine Lake.

Nero (54-68).

Nero was but sixteen years old when he began to reign. For three years he was under the influence of his tutor, **Seneca**, the author, and **Burrhus**, the *Praefect* of the Praetorian Guard, and his government was during this period the most respectable of any since the time of Augustus. His masters kept the young Emperor amused, and removed from the cares of state. But he soon became infatuated with an unscrupulous woman, **Poppaea Sabína**, for whom he neglected and finally killed his wife, Octavia.

It would be useless to follow in detail the crimes of Nero from this time. A freedman, **Tigellínus**, became his adviser, and was the real ruler of the Empire. He encouraged his master in all his vices and wickedness. Poppaea died from a kick administered by Nero in anger; Burrhus was disposed of; Agrippína, and Britannicus, the true heir to the throne, were murdered. The wealthy were plundered, and the feelings of his subjects outraged in every conceivable manner. The Emperor appeared in public, contending first as a musician, and afterwards in the sports of the circus.

The great fire of 18 July, 64, which destroyed a large part of the city, was ascribed to him, but without sufficient evidence; and the stories of his conduct during the conflagration are doubtless pure fictions. It was necessary, however, to fix the guilt on someone; so the **Christians**, then a small sect, made up chiefly of the poorer people, were accused of the crime, and persecuted without mercy. They were often enclosed in fagots covered with pitch, and burned alive.

In rebuilding Rome, Nero took every precaution against the recurrence of a conflagration. Broad regular streets replaced the narrow winding alleys. The new houses were limited in height, built partly of hard stone, and protected by open spaces and colonnades. The water supply was also carefully regulated.

In addition to rebuilding the city, Nero gratified his love for the magnificent by erecting a splendid palace, called the **Golden House**.

Its walls were adorned with gold, precious stones, and masterpieces of art from Greece. The grounds around were marvellous in their meadows, lakes, groves, and distant views. In front was a colossal statue of Nero him- self, one hundred and ten feet high.

Conspiracies having been formed in which Seneca and Lucan were implicated, both men were ordered to take their own lives. Nero's life after this became still more infamous. In a tour made in Greece, ne conducted himself so scandalously that even Roman morals were shocked, and Roman patience could endure him no longer. The Governor of Hither Spain, **Galba**, proclaimed himself Emperor, and marched upon Rome. Verginius, the Governor of Upper Germany, also lent his aid to the insurrection. The Senate proclaimed Nero a public enemy, and condemned him to death. He fled from the city and put an end to his life, June 9, 68, just in time to escape capture. His statues were broken down, his name everywhere erased, and his Golden House demolished. With him ended the Claudian line of Emperors.

Lucius Annaeus Seneca (8 b. c.—65 *a. d.*) was born at Corduba in Spain, of a Spanish Roman family, and was educated at Rome. His father was a teacher of rhetoric, a man of wealth and literary attainments. Seneca began to practise at the bar at Rome, and was gaining considerable when in 41 he was banished to Corsica. Eight years later he was recalled to be tutor of the young Nero, then eleven years old. He was Consul in 57, and during the first years of Nero's reign he shared the administration of affairs with the worthy Burrhus. His influence over Nero, while it lasted, was salutary, though often maintained by doubtful means. In course of time Nero began to dislike him, and when Burrhus died his fate was sealed. By the Emperor's command he committed suicide. Opening the veins in his feet and arms, he discoursed with his friends on the brevity of life till death ensued.

Seneca is the most eminent of the writers of his age. He wrote moral essays, philosophical letters, physical treatises, and tragedies. Of the last, the best are *Hercules Furens*, *Phaedra*, and *Medéa*.

GALBA (68-69)—OTHO (69)—VITELLIUS (69)

Galba entered the city as a conqueror, without much trouble, but on account of his parsimony and austerity he soon became unpopular, and was murdered by his mutinous soldiers fifteen days after he reached Rome. He belonged to an old patrician family, and his overthrow was sincerely regretted by the better element in the city.

Otho, the first husband of Poppaea, and the leader in the insurrection against Galba, was now declared Emperor. No sooner did the news of his accession reach Gaul than **Vitellius**, a general of the army of the Rhine, revolted. Otho marched against the rebels, was defeated, and committed suicide after a reign of three months.

Vitellius had been a good soldier, but as a ruler he was weak and incapable. He was killed after a reign of less than a year, during which he had distinguished himself by gluttony and vulgar sensuality.

CHAPTER 39

The Flavian Emperors

VESPASIAN (69-79).

The East now made a claim for the Emperor, and on July 1, 69, the soldiers who were engaged in war against the revolted Jews in Judaea proclaimed as Emperor their commander, **Titus Flavius Vespasiánus**. He left the conduct of the war in charge of his son Titus, and arrived at Rome in 70. Here he overthrew and put to death Vitellius. In the course of this struggle the Capitol was burned. This he restored, rebuilding also a large part of the city.

In his own life Vespasian was simple, putting to shame the luxury and extravagance of the nobles, and causing a marked improvement in the general tone of society. He removed from the Senate many improper members, replacing them by able men, among whom was **Agricola**. In 70 he put down a formidable rebellion in Gaul; and when his son Titus returned from the capture of Jerusalem,[1] they enjoyed a joint triumph. The Temple of Janus was closed, and peace prevailed during the remainder of his reign.

Much money was spent on public works, and in beautifying the city. A new Forum was built, a Temple of Peace, public baths, and the famous **Colosséum** was begun, receiving its name from the Colossus, a statue of Nero, which had stood nearby.

On the whole, Vespasian was active and prudent in public affairs, frugal and virtuous in private life. The decade of his reign was marked by peace and general prosperity.

One of the ablest men of this age was **Agricola** (37-93). Born at

---

1. Jerusalem was taken in 70, after a siege of several months, the horrors of which have been graphically detailed by the Jewish historian Josephus, who was present in the army of Titus. The city was destroyed, and the inhabitants sold into slavery.

Forum Julii in Gaul, he was made Governor of Aquitania by Vespasian in 73. Four years later he was Consul, and the next year was sent to Britain, which he conquered, and governed with marked ability and moderation, increasing the prosperity of the people and advancing their civilization. He remained in Britain until 85, when he was re-called. His life was written by his son-in-law, the historian Tacitus.

TITUS (79-81).

Vespasian was succeeded by his son **Titus**, who emulated the vir-tues of his father. He finished the Colosséum, begun by Vespasian, and built a triumphal arch to commemorate his victories over the Jews. This arch, called the **Arch of Titus**, was built on the highest part of the Via Sacra, and on its walls was carved a representation of the sacred candlestick of the Jewish temple, which can still be seen.

It was during this reign that **Herculaneum** and **Pompeii** were destroyed by an eruption of Vesuvius. In this eruption perished **Pliny the Elder**, the most noted writer of his day. His work on *Natural History*, the only one of his writings that is preserved, shows that he was a true student. His passion for investigation led him to approach too near the volcano, and caused his death.

DOMITIAN (81-96).

Domitian was the opposite of his brother Titus,—cruel, passion-ate, and extravagant. He was murdered after a reign of fifteen years, during which he earned the hatred and contempt of his subjects by his crimes and inconsistencies.

In his foreign policy Domitian showed considerable ability. He added to the Empire that part of Germany which corresponds to modern Baden and Wirtemberg, and built a line of fortifications from Mentz on the Rhine to Ratisbon on the Danube.

With him ended the line of the **Flavian Emperors**, and he was also the last of the so called **Twelve Caesars**, a name given them by the historian Suetonius.

CHAPTER 40

The Five Good Emperors

NERVA (96-98).

Nerva was appointed by the Senate to succeed Domitian, and was the first Emperor who did not owe his advancement to military force or influence. He associated with himself **Marcus Ulpius Trajánus**, then in command of the army on the Rhine. Nerva ruled only sixteen months; but during that time he restored tranquillity among the people, conferring happiness and prosperity upon every class.

TRAJAN (98-117).

Nerva was succeeded by **Trajan**, whose character has its surest guaranty in the love and veneration of his subjects; and it is said that, long afterwards, the highest praise that could be bestowed on a ruler was that he was "more fortunate than Augustus, and better than Trajan." Trajan was a soldier; and, if he lacked the refinements of a peaceful life, he was nevertheless a wise and firm master.

He added to the Empire Dacia, the country included between the Danube and the Theiss, the Carpathians and the Pruth. This territory became so thoroughly Romanized that the language of its inhabitants today is founded on that of their conquerors nearly eighteen centuries ago. It was in honour of this campaign into Dacia that the famous **Column of Trajan**, which still remains, was erected.

Trajan also annexed to the Empire Arabia Petraea, which afforded an important route between Egypt arid Syria. His invasion of Parthia, however, resulted in no permanent advantage.

During the reign of Trajan the Roman Empire **reached the summit of its power**; but the first signs of decay were beginning to be seen in the financial distress of all Italy, and the decline of the free peasantry, until in the next century they were reduced to a condition of practical serfdom.

The literature of Trajan's reign was second only to that of the Augustan age. His time has often been called the **Silver Age**. Its prose writers were, however, unlike those of the Augustan age, far superior to its poets. The most famous prose writers were **Tacitus, Pliny the Younger**, and **Quintilian**.

The poets of this period were **Juvenal, Persius, Martial, Lucan**, and **Statius**, of whom the last two were of an inferior order.

HADRIAN (117–138)

Trajan was succeeded by his cousin's son, **Hadrian**, a native of Spain. One of the first acts of Hadrian was to relinquish the recent conquests of Trajan, and to restore the old boundaries of the Empire. The reasons for this were that they had reached the utmost limits which could lend strength to the power of Rome, or be held in subjection without constant and expensive military operations. The people occupying the new conquests were hardy and warlike, scattered over a country easy of defence, and certain to strive constantly against a foreign yoke.

Hadrian displayed constant activity in travelling over the Empire, to overlook personally its administration and protection. He visited Britain, where he crushed the inroads of the Caledonians, and built a fortified line of works, known as the **Picts' Wall**, extending from sea to sea. The remains of this great work are still to be seen, corresponding nearly to the modern boundary between England and Scotland. He also visited the East, where the Jews were making serious trouble, and completed their overthrow.

On his return to the city, the Emperor devoted himself to its adornment. Several of his works, more or less complete, still remain. The most famous of these is the **Mausoléum** (Tomb) **of Hadrian**, now known as the Castle of San Angelo.

Hadrian was afflicted with bad health, suffering much from diseases from which he could find no relief. On account of this, and to secure a proper succession, he associated with himself in the government **Titus Aurelius Antonínus**, and required him to adopt Marcus Annius Verus and Lucius Verus. In 138, soon after this arrangement was made, Hadrian died, leaving the Empire to Titus.

TITUS AURELIUS ANTONÍNUS PIUS (138–161).

Antonínus, a native of Gaul, was fifty-two years old when he succeeded to the throne. The cognomen **Pius** was conferred upon him by the Senate on account of the affectionate respect which he had shown for Hadrian. He was a man of noble appearance, firm and prudent, and under him the affairs of state moved smoothly.

MARCUS AURELIUS ANTONÍNUS (161-180).

On the death of Antonínus, Marcus Annius Verus succeeded him under the title of **Marcus Aurelius Antonínus**.

The Moors made an invasion into Spain; the barbarians broke into Gaul; the army in Britain attempted to set up another Emperor; and the Parthians in the East were in an uneasy state. The Eastern war, however, ended favourably, and the Parthian king purchased peace by ceding Mesopotamia to Rome. But the returning army brought with it a pestilence, which spread devastation throughout the West. The Christians were charged with being the cause of the plague, and were cruelly persecuted. Among the victims were **Justin Martyr** at Rome, and **Polycarp** at Smyrna.

The death of Lucius Verus in 168 released Aurelius from a colleague who attracted attention only by his unfitness for his position. The Emperor was thus relieved of embarrassments which might well have become his greatest danger. The remainder of his reign, however, was scarcely less unhappy.

The dangers from the troublesome barbarians grew greater and greater. Rome had now passed the age of conquest, and began to show inability even to defend what she had acquired. For fourteen years Aurelius was engaged on the frontiers fighting these barbarians, and endeavouring to check their advance. He died at Vienna while thus occupied, in the fifty-ninth year of his life (180).

Peace was shortly afterwards made with the barbarians,—a peace bought with money; an example often followed in later times, when Rome lacked the strength and courage to enforce her wishes by force of arms.

Marcus Aurelius was the **Philosopher** of the Empire. His tastes were quiet; he was unassuming, and intent on the good of the people. His faults were amiable weaknesses; his virtues, those of a hero. His *Meditations* have made him known as an author of find tastes and thoughts. With him ended the line of the **Good Emperors**. After his death, Rome's prosperity and power began rapidly to wane.

THE CHRISTIANS.

The **Christians**, who were gradually increasing in numbers, were persecuted at different times throughout the Empire. One ground for these persecutions was that it was a crime against the state to refuse to worship the gods of the Romans under whom the Empire had flourished. It was also the custom to burn incense in front of the Emperor's statue, as an act of adoration. The Christians not only refused homage to the Roman gods, but denounced the burning of incense as sacrilegious. **Aurelius** gave his sanction to the most general persecution this sect had yet suffered. The last combined effort to suppress them was under **Diocletian**, in 284, but it ended with the **Edict of Milan** in 312, which famous decree gave the imperial license to the religion of Christ.

Chapter 41

Period of Military Despotism—
Decline of the Empire

Commodus (180-192).

On the death of Aurelius, his son, **Commodus**, hastened to Rome, and was received by both the Senate and army without opposition. His character was the opposite of that of his good father. In ferocity and vindictiveness he was almost unequalled, even among the Emperors of unhappy Rome. By means of informers, who were well paid, he rid himself of the best members of the Senate. His government became so corrupt, he himself so notorious in crime, that he was unendurable. His proudest boasts were of his triumphs in the amphitheatre, and of his ability to kill a hundred lions with as many arrows. After a reign of twelve years his servants rid the Empire of his presence.

Pertinax (192-193).

Pertinax, the *Praefect* of the city, an old and experienced Senator, followed Commodus. His reign of three months was well meant, but as it was not supported by the military it was of no effect. His attempted reforms were stopped by his murder.

Juliánus (193).—Septimius Sevérus (193-211).

The Praetorians now offered the crown to the highest bidder, who proved to be **Didius Juliánus**, a wealthy Senator. He paid about a thousand dollars to each soldier of the Guard, twelve thousand in number. After enjoying the costly honour two months he was deposed and executed.

In the mean time several soldiers had been declared Emperor by their respective armies. Among them was **Septimius Sevérus**, an African, belonging to the army of the Danube.

Sevérus was an able soldier. He disarmed the Praetorians, banished them from Rome, and filled their place with fifty thousand legionaries, who acted as his body guard. The person whom he placed in command of this guard was made to rank next to himself, with legislative, judicial, and financial powers. The Senate he reduced to a nonentity.

After securing the capital, Sevérus carried on a campaign against the Parthians, and was victorious over the rulers of Mesopotamia and Arabia. In 203 he erected, in commemoration of these victories, a magnificent arch, which still stands at the head of the Forum. He died at Eboracum (York), in Britain, while making preparations for a campaign against the Caledonians.

CARACALLA, MACRINUS, AND HELIOGABALUS.

Sevérus left two sons, both of whom he had associated with himself in the government. No sooner was he dead than they quarrelled, and the elder, **Caracalla**, murdered the other with his own hand in the presence of their mother.

Caracalla was blood-thirsty and cruel. After a short reign (211-216) he was murdered by one of his soldiers. By him were begun the famous baths which bore his name, and of which extensive remains still exist. Caracalla was succeeded by **Macrínus**, who reigned but one year, and was followed by **Heliogabalus** (218-222), a priest of the sun, a true Oriental, with but few virtues. His end was like that of his predecessors. The Praetorians revolted and murdered him.

From Alexander Sevérus to the Age of the Thirty Tyrants (222-268).

Alexander Sevérus was a good man, and well educated. But he endeavoured in vain to check the decline of the state. The military had become all powerful, and he could effect nothing against it. During his reign (222-235), the famous baths begun by Caracalla were finished.

Sevérus was killed in a mutiny led by **Maximin**, who was Emperor for three years (235-238), and was then murdered by his mutinous soldiers.

Gordian, his successor (238-244), was also slain by his own soldiers in his camp on the Euphrátes, and **Philip** (244-249) and **Decius** (249-251) both fell in battle. Under Decius was begun a persecution of the Christians severer than any that preceded it.

The next seventeen years (251-268) is a period of great confusion.

163

Several generals in different provinces were declared Emperor. The Empire nearly fell to pieces, but finally rallied without loss of territory. Its weakness, however, was apparent to all. This period is often called the **Age of the Thirty Tyrants**.

FIVE GOOD EMPERORS (268-283).

Five Good Emperors now ruled and revived somewhat the shattered strength of the government: **Claudius** (268-270); **Aurelian** (270-275); **Tacitus** (275-276); **Probus** (276-282); and **Carus** (282-283). Aurelian undertook a campaign against the famous **Zenobia**, Queen of **Palmýra**. In her he found a worthy foe, one whose political ability was rendered more brilliant by her justice and courage. Defeated in the field, she fortified herself in Palmýra, which was taken after a siege and destroyed. Zenobia was carried to Rome, where she graced the triumph of her conqueror, but was afterwards permitted to live in retirement. Aurelian was the first who built the walls of Rome in their present position.

DIOCLETIAN (284-305).

With this ruler, the last vestige of the old republican form of government at Rome disappears. Old Rome was dead. Her Senate had lost the last remnant of its respectability. Seeing the necessity of a more united country and a firmer rule, Diocletian associated with himself **Maximian**, a gigantic soldier, who signalized his accession by subduing a dangerous revolt in Gaul. He also appointed two officers, **Galerius** and **Constantius**, whom he called **Caesars**,—one to have charge of the East, and the other of the West. By means of these assistants he crushed all revolts, strengthened the waning power of the Empire, and imposed peace and good order upon the world.

Diocletian and Maximian afterwards resigned, and allowed their two Caesars to assume the rank of **Augusti**, and they in their turn appointed Caesars as assistants.

Soon after his accession Constantius died, and his son **Constantine** was proclaimed Caesar, against the wishes of Galerius. A bitter struggle followed, in which Constantine finally overcame all his opponents, and was declared sole Emperor. For his successes he was named the **Great**.

CONSTANTINE THE GREAT (306-337).

Constantine determined to build for his Empire a new capital, which should be worthy of him. He selected the site of **Byzantium** as offering the greatest advantages; for, being defended on three sides by the sea and the Golden Horn, it could easily be made almost impregnable, while as a seaport its advantages were unrivalled,—a feature not in the least shared by Rome. The project was entered upon with energy; the city was built, and named **Constantinople**. To people it, the seat of government was permanently removed thither, and every inducement was offered to immigration. Thus was born the **Greek Empire**, destined to drag out a miserable existence for nearly a thousand years after Rome had fallen a prey to the barbarians. Its founder died, after a reign of thirty years, in his sixty-fourth year (337).

Constantine is entitled to great credit for the uniform kindness with which he treated his Christian subjects. It is said that his mother, **Helena**, was a Christian, and that it was to her influence that this mildness was due. The sect, notwithstanding many persecutions, had kept on increasing, until now we find them a numerous and quite influential body. It was during his reign that the **Decree of Milan** was issued, in 313, giving the imperial license to the religion of Christ; and also in this reign the famous **Council of Nice**, in Bithynia (325), met to settle questions of creed.

In person Constantine was tall and majestic; he was dexterous in all warlike accomplishments; intrepid in war, affable in peace; patient and prudent in council, bold and unhesitating in action. Ambition alone led him to attack the East; and the very madness of jealousy marked his course after his success. He was filial in his affection towards his mother; but he can scarcely be called affectionate who put to death his father-in-law, his brother-in-law, his wife, and his son. If he was great in his virtues, in his faults he was contemptible.

DECLINE OF THE EMPIRE.

Constantine was succeeded by his three sons, **Constantine II.**, **Constantius**, and **Constans**, who divided the Empire among themselves (337-353). Constantine and Constans almost at once quarrelled over the possession of Italy, and the difficulty was ended only by the death of the former. The other two brothers lived in harmony for some time, because the Persian war in the East occupied Constantius, while Constans was satisfied with a life of indolence and dissipation. Constans was murdered in 350, and his brother was sole Emperor. He died ten years later, and was succeeded by his cousin, Julian (360-363)

Julian was a good soldier, and a man calculated to win the love and respect of all. But he attempted to restore the old religion, and thus gained for himself the epithet of **Apostate**. The Christians, however, had too firm a hold on the state to admit of their powers being shaken. The failure of Julian precluded any similar attempt afterward. After a reign of three years, he was killed in an expedition against the Persians. His successor, **Jovian** (363-364), who was chosen by the army, died after a reign of only seven months.

Valentinian and **Valens** (364-375). After a brief *inter-regnum,* the throne was bestowed on Valentinian, who associated with himself his brother Valens. The Empire was divided. Valens took the East, with Constantinople as his capital. Valentinian took the West, making **Milan** the seat of his government. So completely had Rome fallen from her ancient position, that it is very doubtful if this monarch ever visited the city during his reign.[1] He died during a campaign on the Danube. His son **Gratian** (375-383) succeeded him. He discouraged Paganism, and under him Christianity made rapid strides. His uncle Valens was slain in a battle against the Goths; but so completely were the Eastern and Western Empires now separated, that Gratian did not attempt, to make himself sole ruler, but appointed **Theodosius** to the empty throne. Gratian, like so many of his predecessors, was murdered. His successors, **Maximus** (383-388), **Valentinian II.** (388-392), and **Eugenius** (392-394), were either deposed or assassinated, and again there was, for a short time, one ruler of the whole Empire, **Theodosius**, whom Gratian had made Emperor of the East. He was sole Emperor for one year (394-395). On his death his two sons divided the Empire, **Honorius** (395-423) taking the West, and Arcadius the East.

Honorius was only six years old when he began to reign. He was placed under the care of a Vandal named **Stilicho**, to whom he was allied by marriage. Stilicho was a man of ability. The barbarians were driven from the frontiers on the Rhine and in Britain; a revolt in Africa was suppressed. Honorius himself was weak and jealous. He did not hesitate to murder Stilicho as soon as he was old enough to see the power he was wielding. With Stilicho's death his fortune departed. Rome was besieged, captured, and sacked by the barbarian **Alaric**, in 410. When this evil was past, numerous contestants arose in different parts of the Empire, each eager for a portion of the fabric which was now so obviously crumbling to pieces.

Honorius was succeeded, after one of the longest reigns of the

---

1. Since the building of Constantinople no Emperor had lived in Rome. She had ceased to be mistress even of the West, and rapidly fell to the rank of a provincial city.

imperial line, by **Valentinian III.** (423-455). The Empire was but a relic of its former self. Gaul, Spain, and Britain were practically lost; Illyria and Pannonia were in the hands of the Goths; and Africa was soon after seized by the barbarians. Valentinian was fortunate in the possession of **Aetius**, a Scythian by birth, who for a time upheld the Roman name, winning for himself the title of **Last of the Romans**. He was assassinated by his ungrateful master. A few months later, in 455, the Emperor himself was killed by a Senator, **Maximus**, who succeeded him, but for only three months, when **Avítus** (455-456), a noble of Gaul, became Emperor. He was deposed by **Ricimer** (457-467), a Sueve, of considerable ability, who for some time managed the affairs of the Empire, making and unmaking its monarchs at pleasure. After the removal of Avítus, ten months were allowed to elapse before a successor was appointed; and then the crown was bestowed upon **Majorian** (457-461). **Severus** followed him, a man too weak to interfere with the plans of Ricimer.

After his death, Ricimer ruled under the title of **Patrician**, until the people demanded an Emperor, and he appointed **Anthemius** (467-472), who attempted to strengthen his position by marrying a daughter of Ricimer; but jealousy soon sprang up between them. Ricimer invited a horde of barbarians from across the Alps, with whom he captured and sacked Rome, and killed Anthemius. Shortly after, Ricimer himself died.

Names which appear only as names now follow each other in rapid succession. Finally, in 476, **Zeno**, Emperor of the East, declared the office of **Emperor of the West** abolished, and gave the government of the **Diocese of Italy** to **Odoacer**, with the title of Patrician.

CHAPTER 42

Invasions and Distribution of the Barbarians.

The sieges and captures of Rome by the Barbarians we present in a separate chapter, instead of in the narrative of the Emperors, because by this plan a better idea of the operations can be given; and especially because we can thus obtain a clearer and more comprehensive conception of the rise of the nations, which, tearing in pieces the Roman Empire, have made up Modern Europe.

The **Huns**, who originated the movement which overthrew the Western Empire, came, it is supposed, from the eastern part of Asia. As they moved westward, their march was irresistible. In 395 they met and defeated the **Goths**, a powerful tribe that lived to the north of the Danube, and who were ruled by a king named Hermanric.

The Gothic nation consisted of two branches, the **Ostrogoths**, Eastern Goths, and the **Visigoths**, Western Goths. Of these the Ostrogoths were the more powerful, but on the approach of the Huns they were obliged to submit. The Huns moved on, and found but little trouble in overrunning the country of the Visigoths, who were so terrified by the hideous appearance and wild shouts of the Huns that they fled to the Danube, and besought the Romans to allow them to cross the river and take refuge in their territory. The favour was granted, but the refugees were treated with indignity, and compelled to undergo every privation.

Subsequently a remnant of the Ostrogoths arrived at the Danube, also desiring to cross. To them permission was refused, but they seized shipping and crossed, despite the prohibition of the Romans. They found the condition of their brethren, the Visigoths, so sad, that they united with them in open revolt, defeated a Roman army sent against them, and ravaged Thrace. The Emperor Valens took the field in person, and was defeated (378). The Goths then moved southward and westward into Greece, everywhere pillaging the country.

When Theodosius became Emperor, he acted cautiously, fortifying strong points from which to watch the enemy and select a favourable moment for an attack. At length he surprised their camp and gained a complete victory. The Goths were taken into the service of the Empire, and the first chapter of the barbarian invasion of the Empire was brought to a close.

We now meet two of the great names connected with the fall of Rome, **Alaric** and **Stilicho**.

Theodosius was succeeded by Arcadius, and before the end of the year the Goths broke into open revolt under their leader, Alaric. Athens was compelled to pay a ransom; Corinth, Argos, and Sparta were taken and plundered. No place was strong enough to offer effectual resistance. At this juncture, Stilicho, General of the Western Empire, hastened to the scene, and succeeded in surrounding the Goths, but Alaric burst through his lines and escaped. He then made peace with Constantinople, and the office of Master-General of Illyricum was bestowed upon him. How sincere the barbarian was in his offers of peace may be seen from the fact that in two years he invaded Italy (400).

Honorius, who was then Emperor of the West, was a man so weak that even the genius of Stilicho could not save him. No sooner did he hear of the approach of Alaric, than he hastened to a place of safety for himself, leaving Stilicho to defend Rome. Troops were called from Britain, Gaul, and the other provinces far and near, leaving their places vacant and defenceless. Honorius, who had attempted to escape to Gaul, was surprised by Alaric, and, taking refuge in the fortified town of Asta, was there besieged until the arrival of the brave Stilicho, who attacked the besiegers, and after a bloody fight utterly routed them. In his retreat, Alaric attempted to attack Veróna, but he was again defeated, and escaped only by the fleetness of his horse. Honorius returned home (404), and enjoyed a triumph.

Rome had scarcely time to congratulate herself upon her escape from the Goths, when she was threatened by a new enemy.

The Huns, pushing westward, had dislodged the northern tribes of Germany who dwelt on the Baltic. These were the Alans, Sueves, Vandals, and Burgundians. Under the leadership of **Radagaisus**, these tribes invaded Italy with about two hundred thousand men. They were met near Florence by Stilicho, and totally defeated (406). Radagaisus himself was killed. The survivors turned backward, burst into Gaul, ravaged the lower portion of the country, and finally separated. One portion, the Burgundians, remained on the frontier, and from their descendants comes the name of Burgundy.

The Alans, Sueves, and Vandals pushed on into Spain, where they established kingdoms. The Alans occupied the country at the foot of the Pyrenees, but were soon after subdued by the Visigoths. The Sueves settled in the north-west of Spain, but met the same fate as the Alans. The Vandals occupied the southern part, and from there crossed over to Africa, where they maintained themselves for nearly a century, and at one time were powerful enough, as we shall see, to capture Rome itself.

Rome was now for a time delivered from her enemies, and the Emperor, no longer needing Stilicho, was easily persuaded that he was plotting for the throne. He was put to death, with many of his friends.

With Stilicho Rome fell. Scarcely two months after his death, Alaric again appeared before Rome. He sought to starve the city into submission. Famine and pestilence raged within its walls. Finally peace was purchased by a large ransom, and Alaric withdrew, but soon returned. The city was betrayed, and after a lapse of eight centuries became the second time a prey to the barbarians (24 August, 410).

The city was plundered for five days, and then Alaric withdrew to ravage the surrounding country. But the days of this great leader were almost spent. Before the end of the year he died, and shortly after his army marched into France, where they established a kingdom reaching from the Loire and the Rhone to the Straits of Gibraltar.

The **Germans**, under their king, **Clodion**, prompted by the example of the Burgundians and Visigoths, began, about 425, a series of attempts to enlarge their boundaries. They succeeded in establishing themselves firmly in all the country from the Rhine to the Somme, and under the name of **Franks** founded the present French nation in France (447).

Clodion left two sons, who quarrelled over the succession. The elder appealed to the Huns for support, the younger to Rome.

The Huns at this time were ruled by **Attila**, "the Scourge of God." The portrait of this monster is thus painted. His features bore the mark of his Eastern origin. He had a large head, a swarthy complexion, small deep-seated eyes, a flat nose, a few hairs in the place of a beard, broad shoulders, and a short square body, of nervous strength though disproportioned form. This man wielded at will, it is said, an army of over half a million troops.

At the time he received from the son of Clodion the invitation to interfere in the affairs of Gaul, Attila was already contemplating an invasion of both the Western and Eastern Empires; but the prospect of an ally in Gaul, with an opportunity of afterwards attacking Italy from the west, was too favourable to be neglected.

A march of six hundred miles brought the Huns to the Rhine. Crossing this, they continued their progress, sacking and burning whatever cities lay in their route.

The Visigoths under Theodoric, joining the Romans under Aetius, met the Huns near Orleans. Attila retreated towards Chalons, where, in 451, was fought a great battle, which saved the civilization of Western Europe. Attila began the attack. He was bravely met by the Romans; and a charge of the Visigoths completed the discomfiture of the savages. Aetius did not push his victory, but allowed the Huns to retreat in the direction of Italy. The "Scourge" first attacked, captured, and rased to the ground Aquileia. He then scoured the whole country, sparing only those who preserved their lives by the surrender of their wealth.

It was to this invasion that **Venice** owed its rise The inhabitants, who fled from the approach of the Huns, found on the islands in the lagoons at the head of the Adriatic a harbour of safety.

Attila died shortly after (453) from the bursting of a blood-vessel, and with his death the empire of the Huns ceased to exist.

The **Vandals**, we have seen, had established themselves in Africa. They were now ruled by **Genseric**. Carthage was their headquarters, and they were continually ravaging the coasts of the Mediterranean with their fleets.

Maximus, Emperor of Rome (455), had forcibly married Eudoxia, the widow of the previous Emperor, Valentinian, whom he had killed. She in revenge sent to Genseric a secret message to attack Rome. He at once set sail for the mouth of the Tiber. The capital was delivered into his hands on his promise to spare the property of the Church (June, 455), and for fourteen days the Vandals ravaged it at pleasure. Genseric then left Rome, taking with him Eudoxia.

This was the last sack of the city by barbarians. But twenty-one years elapsed before the Roman Empire came to an end (476).

CHAPTER 43

Roman Literature

PLAUTUS (254-184).

Plautus, the comic poet, was one of the earliest of Roman writers. Born at Sarsina in Umbria, of free parentage, he at first worked on the stage at Rome, but lost his savings in speculation. Then for some time he worked in a treadmill, but finally gained a living by translating Greek comedies into Latin. Twenty of his plays have come down to us. They are lively, graphic, and full of fun, depicting a mixture of Greek and Roman life.

TERENCE (195-159).

Terence was a native of Carthage. He was brought to Rome at an early age as a slave of the Senator Terentius, by whom he was educated and liberated. Six of his comedies are preserved. Like the plays of Plautus, they are free translations from the Greek, and of the same general character.

ENNIUS (239-169).

Quintus Ennius, a native of Rudiae, was taken to Rome by Cato the Younger. Here he supported himself by teaching Greek. His epic poem, the *Annáles*, relates the traditional Roman history, from the arrival of Aenéas to the poet's own day.

CICERO (106-43).

Marcus Tullius Cicero, a native of Arpínum, ranks as the first prose writer in Roman literature. As an orator Cicero had a very happy natural talent. The extreme versatility of his mind, his lively imagination, his great sensitiveness, his inexhaustible richness of expression, which was never at a loss for a word or tone to suit any circumstances or mood, his felicitous memory, his splendid voice and impressive figure, all contributed to render him a powerful speaker. He himself left nothing undone to attain perfection. Not until he had spent a long time in laborious study and preparation did he make his *début* as an orator; nor did he ever rest and think himself perfect, but, always working, made the most careful preparation for every case. Each success was to him only a step to another still higher achievement; and by continual meditation and study he kept himself fully equipped for his task. Hence he succeeded, as is universally admitted, in gaining a place beside Demosthenes, or at all events second only to him.

There are. extant fifty-seven orations of Cicero, and fragments of twenty more. His famous *Philippics* against Antony caused his proscription by the Second Triumvirate, and his murder near his villa at Formiae, in December, 43.

His chief writings on rhetoric were *De Oratore*; *Brutus de Claris Oratoribus*; and *Orator ad M. Brutum.* Cicero was a lover of philosophy, and his writings on the subject were numerous. Those most read are *De Senectute*, *De Amicitia*, and *De Officiis.*

Eight hundred and sixty-four of Cicero's letters are extant, furnish an inexhaustible treasure of contemporaneous history. (See chapters 27 and 35).

CAESAR (100–44).

Of **Caesar's** literary works the most important are his *Commentarii*, containing the history of the first seven years of the Gallic war, and the history of the civil strife down to the Alexandrine war. The account of his last year in Gaul was written probably by Aulus Hirtius; that of the Alexandrine, African, and Spanish wars, by some unknown hand. As an orator, Caesar ranks next to Cicero.

NEPOS (94–24).

Cornelius Nepos, a native of Northern Italy, was a friend of both Cicero and Atticus. He was a prolific writer, but only his *De Viris Illustribus* is preserved. It shows neither historical accuracy nor good style.

LUCRETIUS (98–55).

Titus Lucretius Carus has left a didactic poem, *De Rerum Natura*, The tone of the work is sad, and in many places bitter.

CATULLUS (87–47).

Gaius Valerius Catullus, of Veróna, is the greatest lyric poet of Roman literature. One hundred and sixteen of his poems are extant.

VIRGIL (70-19).

The great epic Roman poet was **Virgil**. His *Aenéis*, in twelve books, gives an account of the wanderings and adventures of Aenéas, and his struggles to found a city in Italy. The poem was not revised when Virgil died, and it was published contrary to his wishes.

Besides the *Aenéis*, Virgil wrote the *Bucolica*, ten Eclogues imitated and partially translated from the Greek poet Theocritus. The *Georgica*, a poem of four books on agriculture in its different branches, is considered his most finished work, and the most perfect production of Roman art-poetry. (See chapter 37.)

HORACE (65-8).

Quintus Horatius Flaccus left four books of Odes, one of Epodes, two of Satires, two of Epistles, and the *Ars Poetica*. (See chapter 37.)

TIBULLUS (54-29).

Albius Tibullus, an elegiac poet, celebrated in exquisitely fine poems the beauty and cruelty of his mistresses.

PROPERTIUS (49-15).

Sextus Propertius, a native of Umbria, was also an elegiac poet, and wrote mostly on love.

OVID (43 B. C.—18 A. D.)

Publius Ovidius Naso left three books of *Amores*; one of *Heroides*; the *Ars Amatoria*; *Remedia Amoris*; the *Metamorphoses* (fifteen books); the *Tristia*; and the *Fasti*. (See chapter 37.)

LIVY (59 B. C.—17 A .D.).

Titus Livius left a history of Rome, of which thirty-five books have been preserved. (See chapter 37.)

PHAEDRUS.

Phaedrus, a writer of fables, flourished in the reign of Tiberius (14-37). He was originally a slave. His fables are ninety-seven in number, and are written in iambic verse.

SENECA (8 B. C.—65 A. D.)

For an account of this writer see chapter 38, on the Emperor Nero.

CURTIUS.

Quintus Curtius Rufus was a historian who lived in the reign of

Claudius (50 *a. d.*). He wrote a history of the exploits of Alexander the Great.

PERSIUS (34-62).

Persius, a poet of the reign of Nero, was a native of Volaterrae. He wrote six satires, which are obscure and hard to understand.

LUCAN (39-65).

Lucan, a nephew of Seneca, wrote an epic poem (not finished) called *Pharsalia*, upon the civil war between Caesar and Pompey.

PLINY THE ELDER (23-79).

Gaius Plinius Secundus, of Northern Italy, was a great scholar in history, grammar, rhetoric, and natural science. His work on *Natural History* has come down to us.

STATIUS, MARTIAL, QUINTILIAN, JUVENAL.

Statius (45-96), a native of Naples, had considerable poetical talent. He wrote the *Thebaid*, the *Achilleis* (unfinished), and the *Silvae*.

Martial (42-102), wrote sharp and witty epigrams, of which fifteen books are extant. He was a native of Spain.

Quintilian (35-95), was also a native of Spain. He was a teacher of eloquence for many years in Rome. His work *On the Training of an Orator,* is preserved,

Juvenal (47-130), of Aquínum, was a great satirist, who described and attacked bitterly the vices of Roman society. Sixteen of his satires are still in existence.

TACITUS (54-119).

Cornelius Tacitus was the great historian of his age. His birthplace is unknown. His writings are interesting and of a high tone, but often tinged with prejudice, and hence unfair. He wrote,—

1. A dialogue on orators.
2. A biography of his father-in-law, Agricola.
3. A description of the habits of the people of Germany.
4. A history of the reigns of Galba, Otho, Vespasian, Titus, and Domitian (*Historiae*).
5. *Annàles*, a narrative of the events of the reigns of Tiberius, Caligula, Claudius, and Nero.

PLINY THE YOUNGER (62-113).

Pliny the Younger was the adopted son of Pliny the Elder. He was a voluminous correspondent We have nine books of his letters, relating to a large number of subjects, and presenting vivid pictures of the times in which he lived. Their diction is fluent and smooth.

CHAPTER 44

Roman Roads—Provinces

The Romans were famous for their excellent public roads, from thirteen to fifteen feet wide. The road-bed was formed of four distinct layers, placed above the foundation. The upper layer was made of large polygonal blocks of the hardest stone, fitted and joined together so as to make an even surface. On each side of the road were footpaths strewn with gravel. Stone blocks for the use of equestrians were at regular distances, and also milestones telling the distance from Rome. There were four main public roads:—

1. **Via Appia**, from Rome to Capua, Beneventum, Tarentum, and Brundisium.

2. **Via Latína**, from Rome to Aquínum and Teánum, joining the Via Appia at Beneventum.

3. **Via Flaminia**, the great northern road. In Umbria, near Ocriculum and Narnia, a branch went east through Spoletium, joining the main line at Fulsinia. It then continued through Fanum, Flaminii, and Nuceria, where it again divided, one branch going to Fanum Fortúnae on the Adriatic, the other to Ancóna, and from there along the coast to Fanum Fortúnae, where the two branches, again uniting, passed on to Ariminum through Pisaurum. From here it was extended, under the name of **Via Aemilia**, into the heart of Cisalpine Gaul, through Bononia, Mutina, Parma, and Placentia, where it crossed the Po, to Mediolánum.

4. **Via Aurelia**, the great coast road, reached the west coast at Alsium, following the shore along through Etruria and Liguria, by Genua, as far as Forum Julii, in Gaul.

Provinces.

After the conquest of Italy, all the additional Roman dominions were divided into provinces. Sicily was the first Roman province. At first *Praetors* were appointed to govern these provinces; but afterwards persons who had been Praetors at Rome were appointed at the expiration of their office, with the title of **Propraetor**. Later, the Consuls also, at the end of their year of office, were sent to govern provinces, with the title of **Proconsul**. Such provinces were called *Provinciae Consulàres*. The provinces were generally distributed by lot, but their distribution was sometimes arranged by agreement among those entitled to them. The tenure of office was usually a year, but it was frequently prolonged. When a new governor arrived in the province, his predecessor was expected to leave within thirty days.

The governor was assisted by two *Quaestors*, who had charge of the financial duties of the government. Originally the governor was obliged to account at Rome for his administration, from his own books and those of the **Quaestors**; but after 61 b.c, he was obliged to deposit two copies of his, accounts in the two chief cities of his province, and to forward a third to Rome.

If the governor misconducted himself in the performance of his official duties, the provincials might apply for redress to the Senate, and to influential Romans who were their patrons.

The governor received no salary, but was allowed to exact certain contributions from the people of the province for the support of himself and his retinue, which consisted of *quaestors*, secretary, notary, *lictors*, *augurs*, and public criers. His authority was supreme in military and civil matters, and he could not be removed from office. But after his term had ended, he could be tried for mismanagement.

Many of the governors were rascals, and obtained by unfair means vast sums of money from the provincials. One of the most notorious of these was Verres, against whom Cicero delivered his Verrine orations.

At the time of the Battle of Actium there were eighteen provinces; *viz.* Sicilia (227 [1]), Sardinia and Corsica (227), Hispania Citerior (205), Hispania Ulterior (205), Illyricum (167), Macedonia (146), Africa (146), Asia (133), Achaia (146), Gallia Citerior (80), Gallia Narbonensis (118), Cilicia (63), Syria (64), Bithynia and Pontus (63), Cyprus (55), Cyrenaica and Crete (63), Numidia (46), and Mauritania (46).

Under the Emperors the following sixteen were added: Rhoetia,

---

1. The figures in parentheses indicate the date at which the province was established.

Noricum, Pannonia, Moesia, Dacia, Britannia, Aegyptus, Cappadocia, Galatia, Rhodus, Lycia, Judaea, Arabia, Mesopotamia, Armenia, and Assyria.

Roman Officers, etc.

The magistrates of Rome were of two classes; the *Majores*, or higher, and the *Minores*, or lower. The former, except the Censor, had the *Imperium*; the latter did not. To the former class belonged the Consuls, *Praetors*, and Censors, who were all elected in the *Comitia Centuriáta*. The magistrates were also divided into two other classes, *viz. Curule* and Non-*Curule*. The *Curule* offices were those of Dictator, *Magister Equitum*, Consul, *Praetor*, Censor, and *Curule Aedile*. These officers had the right to sit in the *sella curúlis*, chair of state. This chair was displayed upon all public occasions, especially in the circus and theatre; and it was the seat of the Praetor when he administered justice. In shape it was plain, resembling a common folding camp-stool, with crooked legs. It was ornamented with ivory, and later overlaid with gold.

The descendants of anyone who had held a *curule* office were nobles, and had the right to place in their halls and to carry at funeral processions a wax mask of this ancestor, as well as of any other deceased members of the family of *curule* rank.

A person who first held a *curule* office, and whose ancestors had never held one, was called a *novus homo, i.e.* a new man. The most famous new men were Marius and Cicero.

The magistrates were chosen only from the patricians in the early republic; but in course of time the plebeians shared these honours. The plebeian magistrates, properly so called, were the plebeian Aediles and the Tribúni Plebis.

All the magistrates, except the Censor, were elected for one year; and all but the Tribunes and *Quaestors* began their term of office on

---

1 Most of the information given in this chapter is scattered in different parts of the history; but it seems well to condense it into one chapter for readier reference.

January 1st. The Tribune's year began December 10th; that of the *Quaestor*, December 5th.

The offices, except that of Tribune, formed a gradation, through which one must pass if he desired the consulship. The earliest age for holding each was, for the *quaestorship*, twenty-seven years; for the *aedileship*, thirty-seven; for the *praetorship*, forty; and for the consulship, forty-three. No magistrate received any salary, and only the wealthy could afford to hold office.

THE CONSULS.

The two Consuls were the highest magistrates, except when a Dictator was appointed, and were the chiefs of the administration. Their power was equal, and they had the right before all others of summoning the Senate and the *Comitia Centuriáta*, in each of which they presided.

"When both Consuls were in the city, they usually took turns in performing the official duties, each acting a month; and during this time the Consul was always accompanied in public by twelve *lictors*, who preceded him in single file, each carrying on his shoulders a bundle of rods (*fasces*), to signify the power of the magistrate to scourge criminals. Outside the city, these fasces showed an axe projecting from each bundle, signifying the power of the magistrate to behead criminals."

At the expiration of his year of office, the Consul was sent to govern a province for one year, and was then called the *Proconsul*. He was chief in his province in all military, civil, and criminal cases.

PRAETORS.

There were eight *Praetors*, whose duties were to administer justice (judges). After the expiration of their year of office, they went, as *Propraetors*, to govern provinces. The most important *Praetor* was called *Praetor Urbánus*. He had charge of all civil suits between Roman citizens. In the absence of both Consuls from the city, he acted in their place. Each Praetor was attended by two *lictors* in the city, and by six outside. The *Praetor Peregrínus* had charge of civil cases in which one or both parties were aliens. The other six *Praetors* presided over the permanent criminal courts.

AEDILES.

The *Aediles* were four officers who had the general superintendence of the police of the city, and the care of the public games and buildings. Two of the *Aediles* were taken from the plebeians, and two, called *Curule Aediles*, ranked with the higher magistrates, and might be patricians. They were elected in the *Comitia Tribúta*. Their supervision of the public games gave them great opportunities for gaining favour with the populace, who then, as now, delighted in circuses and contests. A small sum was appropriated from the public treasury for these games; but an *Aedile* usually expended much from his own purse to make the show magnificent, and thus to gain; votes for the next office, that of *Praetor*. Only the very wealthy could afford to hold this office.

QUAESTORS.

There were twenty *Quaestors*. Two were city treasurers at Rome, having charge also of the archives. The others were assigned to the different governors of the provinces, and acted as quartermasters. Through their clerks, the two city *Quaestors* kept the accounts, received the taxes, and paid out the city's money, as directed by the Senate. A *Quaestor* always accompanied every *Imperator* (general) in the field as his quartermaster. The elections for *Quaestors* were held in the *Comitia Tribúta*.

TRIBUNI PLEBIS.

There were ten Tribunes, elected in the *Comitia Tribúta*. They were always plebeians, and their chief power lay in their right to veto any decree of the Senate, any law of the *Comitia*, and any public act of a magistrate. Their persons were considered sacred, and no one could hinder them in the discharge of their official duties under penalty of death. They called together the *Comitia Tribúta*, and they also had authority to convene the Senate and to preside over it. Sulla succeeded in restricting their power; but Pompey restored it. The Tribunes did not possess the *imperium*.

CENSORS.

There were two Censors, chosen from Ex-Consuls, and they held office for eighteen months. They were elected once every five years, this period being called a *lustrum*. They ranked as higher magistrates without possessing the *imperium*. Their duties were:

(1) To take the census, *i. e.* register the citizens and their amount of property, and to fill all vacancies in the Senate.

(2) To have a general oversight of the finances, like our Secretary of the Treasury; to contract for the erecting of public buildings, and for the making or repairing of public roads, sewers,

etc.; to let out the privilege of collecting the taxes, for five years, to the highest bidder. [1]

(*3*) To punish gross immorality by removal of the guilty parties from the Senate, the *Equites*, or the tribe.

DICTATOR.

In cases of great danger the Senate called upon the Consuls to appoint a Dictator, who should possess supreme power, but whose tenure of office could never exceed six months. In later times Dictators were not appointed, but Consuls were invested with the authority if it was thought necessary. Sulla and Caesar, however, revived the office, but changed its tenure, the latter holding it for life.

MAGISTER EQUTTUM.

This was an officer appointed by the Dictator, to stand next in authority to him, and act as a sort of Vice-Dictator.

PONTIFICES.

The priests formed a body (*collegium*) of fifteen members, at the head of whom was the *Pontifex Maximus* (high priest). Their tenure of office was for life, and they were responsible to no one in the discharge of their duties. Their influence was necessarily very great.

IMPERIUM.

This was a power to command the armies, and to exercise judicial functions conferred upon a magistrate (Dictator, Consul, or *Praetor*) by a special law passed by the *Comitia Curiáta*. The *Imperium* could be exercised only outside of the city walls (*pomoerium*), except by special permission of the Senate for the purpose of celebrating a triumph. The one receiving the *Imperium* was called **Imperator**.

POTESTAS.

This was the power, in general, which *all* magistrates possessed.

---

1 In the intervals of the censorship, the duties under (2) fell to the *Aediles*.

CHAPTER 46

Houses, Customs, Institutions, etc.

The private houses of the Romans were poor affairs until after the conquest of the East, when money began to pour into the city. Many houses of immense size were then erected, adorned with columns, paintings, statues, and costly works of art. Some of these houses are said to have cost as much as two million dollars.

The principal parts of a Roman house were the *Vestibulum, Ostium, Atrium, Alae, Tablinum, Fauces,* and *Peristylium.* The **Vestibulum** was a court surrounded by the house on three sides, and open on the fourth to the street The **Ostium** corresponded in general to our front hall. From it a door opened into the **Atrium**, which was a large room with an opening in the centre of its roof, through which the rain-water was carried into a cistern placed in the floor under the opening. To the right and left of the Atrium were side rooms called the **Alae**, and the **Tablínum** was a balcony attached to it. The passages from the Atrium to the interior of the house were called **Fauces**. The **Peristylium**, towards which these passages ran, was an open court surrounded by columns, decorated with flowers and shrubs. It was somewhat larger than the Atrium.

The floors were covered with stone, marble, or mosaics. The walls were lined with marble slabs, or frescoed, while the ceilings were either bare, exposing the beams, or, in the finer houses, covered with ivory, gold, and *frescoing.*

The main rooms were lighted from above; the side rooms received their light from these, and not through windows looking into the street. The windows of rooms in upper stories were not supplied with glass until the time of the Empire. They were merely openings in the wall, covered with lattice-work. To heat a room, portable stoves were generally used, in which charcoal was burned. There were no chimneys, and the smoke passed out through the windows or the openings in the roofs.

The rooms of the wealthy were furnished with great splendour. The walls were *frescoed* with scenes from Greek mythology, landscapes, etc. In the vestibules were fine sculptures, costly marble walls, and doors ornamented with gold, silver, and rare shells. There were expensive rugs from the East, and, in fact, everything that could be obtained likely to add to the attractiveness of the room.

Candles were used in early times, but later the wealthy used lamps, which were made of *terra-cotta* or bronze. They were mostly oval, flat on the top, often with figures in relief. In them were one or more round holes to admit the wick. They either rested on tables, or were suspended by chains from the ceiling.

MEALS.

The meals were the **Jentaculum**, **Prandium**, and **Coena**. The first was our breakfast, though served at an early hour, sometimes as early as four o'clock. It consisted of bread, cheese, and dried fruits. The *prandium* was a lunch served about noon. The *coena*, or dinner, served between three and sunset, was usually of three courses. The first course consisted of stimulants, eggs, or lettuce and olives; the second, which was the main course, consisted of meats, fowl, or fish, with condiments; the third course was made up of fruits, nuts, sweetmeats, and cakes.

At elaborate dinners the guests assembled, each with his napkin and full dress of bright colours. The shoes were removed so as not to soil the couches. These couches usually were adapted for three guests, who reclined, resting the head on the left hand, with the elbow supported by pillows. The Romans took the food with their fingers. Dinner was served in a room called the **Triclinium**. In Nero's "Golden House," the dining-room was constructed like a theatre, with shifting scenes to change with every course.

DRESS.—BATHING.

The Roman men usually wore two garments, the **Tunica** and **Toga**. The former was a short woollen under garment with short sleeves. To have a long tunic with long sleeves was considered a mark of effeminacy. The tunic was girded round the waist with a belt. The *toga* was peculiarly a Roman garment, and none but citizens were allowed to wear it. It was also the garment of peace, in distinction from the **Sagum**, which was worn by soldiers. The *toga* was of white wool and was nearly semicircular, but being a cumbrous garment, it became customary in later times to wear it only on state occasions. The poor wore only the tunic, others wore, in place of the *toga*, the **Lacerna**, which was an open cloak, fastened to the right shoulder by a buckle. Boys, until about sixteen, wore a *toga* with a purple hem.

The women wore a **Tunic, Stola**, and **Pulla**. The *stola* was a loose garment, gathered in and girdled at the waist with a deep flounce extending to the feet. The *pulla* was a sort of shawl to throw over the whole figure, and to be worn out of doors. The ladies indulged their fancy for ornaments as freely as their purses would allow.

Foot-gear was mostly of two kinds, the **Calceus** and the **Soleae**. The former was much like our shoe, and was worn in the street. The latter were sandals, strapped to the bare foot, and worn in the house. The poor used wooden shoes.

Bathing was popular among the wealthy. Fine buildings were erected, with elegant decorations, and all conveniences for cold, warm, hot, and vapour baths. These bath-houses were very numerous, and were places of popular resort Attached to many of them were rooms for exercise, with seats for spectators. The usual time for bathing was just before dinner. Upon leaving the bath, it was customary to anoint the body with oil.

Festivals, Games, etc

The Saturnalia was the festival of Saturn, to whom the inhabitants of Latium attributed the introduction of agriculture and the arts of civilized life. It was celebrated near the end of December, corresponding to our Christmas holidays, and under the Empire lasted seven days. During its continuance no public business was transacted, the law courts were closed, the schools had a holiday, and slaves were relieved from all ordinary toil. All classes devoted themselves to pleasure, and presents were interchanged among friends.

The **Lupercalia**, a festival in honour of Lupercus, the god of fertility, was celebrated on the 15th of February. It was one of the most ancient festivals, and was held in the Lupercal, where Romulus and Remus were said to have been nursed by the she wolf (*lupa*). The priests of Lupercus were called **Luperci**. They formed a *collegium*, but their tenure of office is not known. On the day of the festival these priests met at the Lupercal, offered sacrifice of goats, and took a meal, with plenty of wine. They then cut up the skins of the goats which they had sacrificed. With some of these they covered parts of their bodies, and with others they made thongs, and, holding them in their hands, ran through the streets of Rome, striking with them all whom they met, especially women, as it was believed this would render them fruitful.

The **Quirínalia** was celebrated on the 17th of February, when Quirínus (Romulus) was said to have been carried up to heaven.

Gladiators were men who fought with swords in the amphitheatre and other places, for the amusement of the people. These shows were first exhibited at Rome in 264 b. c, and were confined to public funerals; but afterwards gladiators were to be seen at the funerals of most men of rank. Under the Empire the passion for this kind of amusement increased to such an extent, that gladiators were kept and trained in schools (*ludi*) and their trainers were called *Lanistae*. The person who gave an exhibition was called an Editor. He published (*edere*), some time before the show, a list of the combatants. In the show the fights began with wooden swords, but at the sound of the trumpet these were exchanged for steel weapons. When a combatant was wounded, if the spectators wished him spared, they held their thumbs down, but turned them up if they wanted him killed. Gladiators who had served a long time, were often discharged and presented with a wooden sword (*rudis*). Hence they were called *rudiarii*.

THE AMPHITHEATRE, THEATRE, AND CIRCUS.

The **Amphitheatre** was a place for the exhibition of gladiatorial shows, combats of wild beasts, and naval engagements. Its shape was that of an ellipse, surrounded by seats for the spectators. The word Amphitheatre was first applied to a wooden building erected by Caesar. Augustus built one of stone in the Campus Martius, but the most celebrated amphitheatre was built by Vespasian and Titus, and dedicated in 80 *a. d.* It is still standing, though partly in ruins, covers nearly six acres, and could seat ninety thousand people. The name given to it today is the **Colosséum**. The open space in the centre was called the **Aréna**, and was surrounded by a wall about fifteen feet high to protect the spectators from the wild beasts. Before the time of Caesar the shows were held in the Forum and in the Circus.

The **Theatre** was never as popular with the Romans as with the Greeks. The plays of Plautus and Terence were acted on temporary wooden stages. The first stone theatre was built by Pompey in 55 b.c. near the Campus Martius. It was a fine building, with a seating capacity of forty thousand. The seats were arranged in a semicircle, as at present, the orchestra being reserved for the Senators and other distinguished persons. Then came fourteen rows of seats for the *Equites*, and behind these sat the ordinary crowd.

The **Circus Maximus**, between the Palatine and Aventine Hills, was built for chariot races, boxing, and gymnastic contests. It was an immense structure, with galleries three stories high, and a canal called Euripus, and it accommodated one hundred thousand spectators. In the centre Caesar erected an obelisk one hundred and thirty-two feet high, brought from Egypt. The seats were arranged as in the theatre. Six kinds of games were celebrated:

1st, chariot racing;
2nd, a sham-fight between young men on horseback;
3rd, a sham-fight between infantry and cavalry;
4th, athletic sports of all kinds;
5th, fights with wild beasts, such as lions, boars, etc.;
6th, sea fights. Water was let into the canal to float ships.

The combatants were captives, or criminals condemned to death, who fought until one party was killed, unless saved by the kindness of the Emperor.

A Triumphal Procession.

The *Imperator*, when he returned from a successful campaign, was sometimes allowed to enjoy a triumphal procession, provided he had been Dictator, Consul, or *Praetor*. No one desiring a triumph ever entered the city until the Senate decided whether or not he deserved one. When a favourable decision was reached, the temples were all thrown open, garlands of flowers decorated every shrine and image, and incense smoked on every altar. The *Imperator* ascended the triumphal car and entered a city gate, where he was met by the whole body of the Senate, headed by the magistrates.

The procession then proceeded in the following order:—

1. The Senate, headed by the magistrates.
2. A troop of trumpeters.
3. Carts laden with spoils, often very costly and numerous.
4. A body of flute-players.
5. White bulls and oxen for sacrifice.
6. Elephants and rare animals from the conquered countries.
7. The arms and insignia of the leaders of the conquered enemy.
8. The leaders themselves, with their relatives and other captives.

9. The *lictors* of the *Imperator* in single file, their *fasces* wreathed with laurel.

10. The *Imperator* himself, in a circular chariot drawn by four horses. He was attired in a gold-embroidered robe, and a flowered tunic; he held a laurel bough in his right hand, a sceptre in his left, and his brow was encircled with a laurel wreath.

11. The grown up sons and officers of the *Imperator*.

12. The whole body of infantry, with spears adorned with laurel.

The **Ovation** was a sort of smaller triumph. The commander entered the city on foot, or in later times on horseback. He was clothed in a purple-bordered robe. His head was crowned with laurel, and a sheep (*ovis*) was sacrificed, instead of a bull as in the case of a triumph.

POMOERIUM.

The **Pomoerium** was the sacred enclosure of the city, inside of which no person holding the *Imperium* was allowed to enter. It did not always run parallel to the city walls.

NAMES.

Every man in Rome had three names. The given name (*praenomen*), as Lucius, Marcus, Gaius. The name of the *gens* (*nomen*), as Cornelius, Tullius, Julius. The name of the family (*cognómen*), as Scipio, Cicero, Caesar. To these names was sometimes added another, the *agnomen*, given for some exploit, or to show that the person was adopted from some other gens. Thus Scipio the elder was called **Africánus**, and all his descendants had the right to the name. Africánus the younger was adopted from the Cornelian *gens* into the Aemilian gens; therefore he added to his other names **Aemiliánus**.

The women were called only by the name of their *gens*. The daughter of Scipio was called, for example, **Cornelia**, and to distinguish her from others of the Cornelian *gens* she was called Cornelia daughter of Scipio. If there were more than one daughter, to the name of the eldest was added *prima* (first), to that of the next, *secunda* (second), etc.

MARRIAGE.

Intermarriage (*connubium*) between patricians and plebeians was forbidden previous to 445, and after that the offspring of such marriages took the rank of the father. After the parties had agreed to marry, and the consent of the parents or persons in authority was given, the marriage contract was drawn up and signed by both parties. The wedding day was then fixed upon. This could not fall upon the *Kalends*, *Nones*, or *Ides* of any month, or upon any day in May or February. The bride was dressed in a long white robe, with a bridal veil, and shoes of a bright yellow colour. She was conducted in the evening to her future husband's home by three boys, one of whom carried before her a torch, the other two supporting her by the arm. They were accompanied by friends of both parties. The groom received the bride at the door, which she entered with distaff and spindle in hand. The keys of the house were then delivered to her. The day ended with a feast given by the husband, after which the bride was conducted to the bridal couch, in the *atrium*, which was adorned with flowers. On the following day another feast was given by the husband, and the wife performed certain religious rites.

The position of the Roman woman after marriage was very different from that of the Greek. She presided over the whole household, educated her children, watched over and preserved the honour of the house, and shared the honours and respect shown to her husband.

FUNERALS.

When a Roman was at the point of death, his nearest relative present endeavoured to catch the last breath with his mouth. The ring was removed from the dying person's hand, and as soon as he was dead his eyes and mouth were closed by the nearest relative, who called upon the deceased by name, exclaiming "Farewell!" The body was then washed, and anointed with oil and perfumes, by slaves or undertakers. A small coin was placed in the mouth of the body to pay the ferryman (Charon) in Hades, and the body was laid out on a couch in the *vestibulum*, with its feet toward the door. In early times all funerals were held at night; but in later times only the poor followed this custom, mainly because they could not afford display. The funeral, held the ninth day after the death, was headed by musicians playing mournful strains, and mourning women hired to lament and sing the funeral song.

These were sometimes followed by players and buffoons, one of whom represented the character of the deceased, and imitated his words and actions. Then came the slaves whom the deceased had liberated, each wearing the cap of liberty. Before the body were carried the images of the dead and of his ancestors, and also the crown and military rewards which he had gained. The couch on which the body was carried was sometimes made of ivory, and covered with gold and purple. Following it were the relatives in mourning, often uttering loud lamentations, the women beating their breasts and tearing their hair.

The procession of the most illustrious dead passed through the Forum, and stopped before the *Rostra*, where a funeral oration was delivered. From here the body was carried to its place of burial, which must be outside the city. Bodies were sometimes cremated, and in the later times of the Republic this became quite common.

EDUCATION.

In early times the education of the Romans was confined to reading, writing, and arithmetic; but as they came in contact with the Greeks a taste for higher education was acquired. Greek slaves (*paedagógi*) were employed in the wealthy families to watch over the children, and to teach them to converse in Greek.

A full course of instruction included the elementary branches mentioned above, and a careful study of the best Greek and Latin writers, besides a course in philosophy and rhetoric, under some well known professor abroad, usually at Athens or Rhodes.

BOOKS.—LETTER WRITING.

The most common material on which books were written was the thin rind of the Egyptian papyrus tree. Besides the papyrus, parchment was often used. The paper or parchment was joined together so as to form one sheet, and was rolled on a staff, whence the name volume (from *volvere*, to roll).

Letter writing was very common among the educated. Letters were usually written with the *stylus*, an iron instrument like a pencil in size and shape, on thin slips of wood or ivory covered with wax, and folded together with the writing on the inside. The slips were tied together by a string, and the knot was sealed with wax and stamped with a signet ring. Letters were also written on parchment with ink. Special messengers were employed to carry letters, as there was no regular mail service. Roman letters differed from ours chiefly in the opening and close. The writer always began by sending "greeting" to the person addressed, and closed with a simple "farewell," without any signature. Thus "Cicero S. D. Pompeio" (S. D. = sends greeting) would be the usual opening of a letter from Cicero to Pompey.

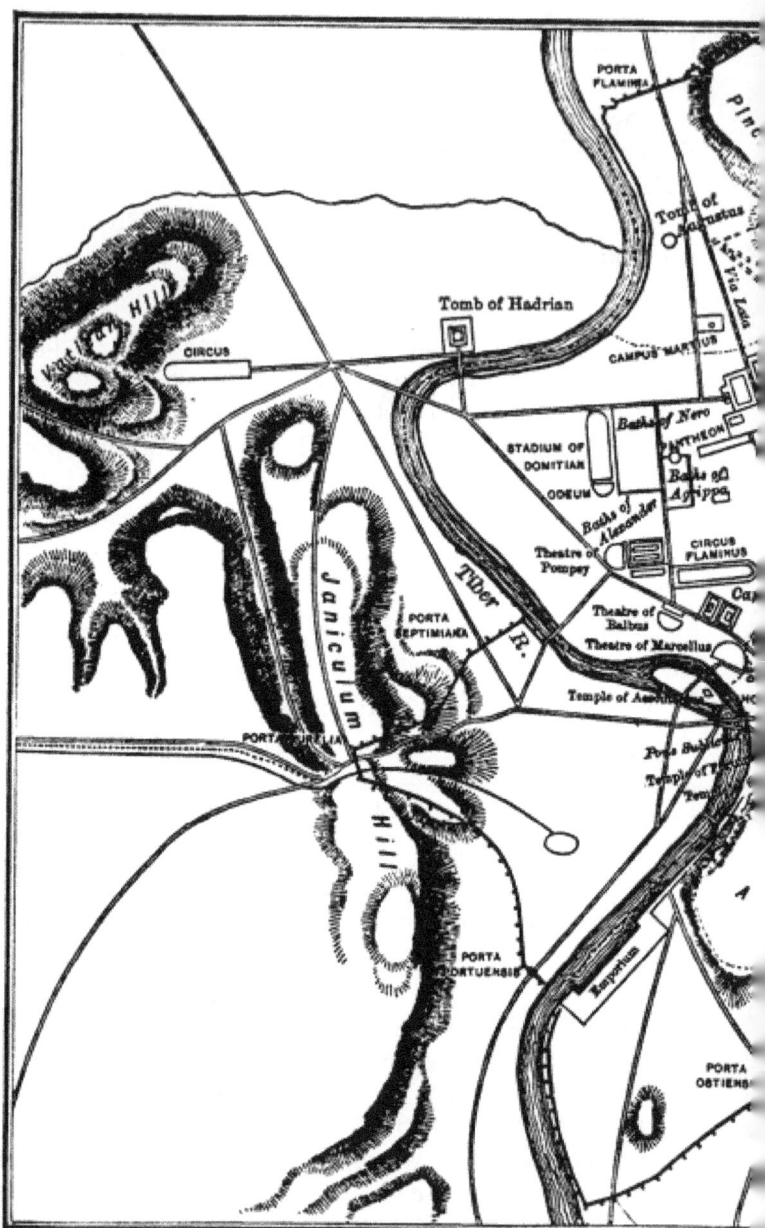

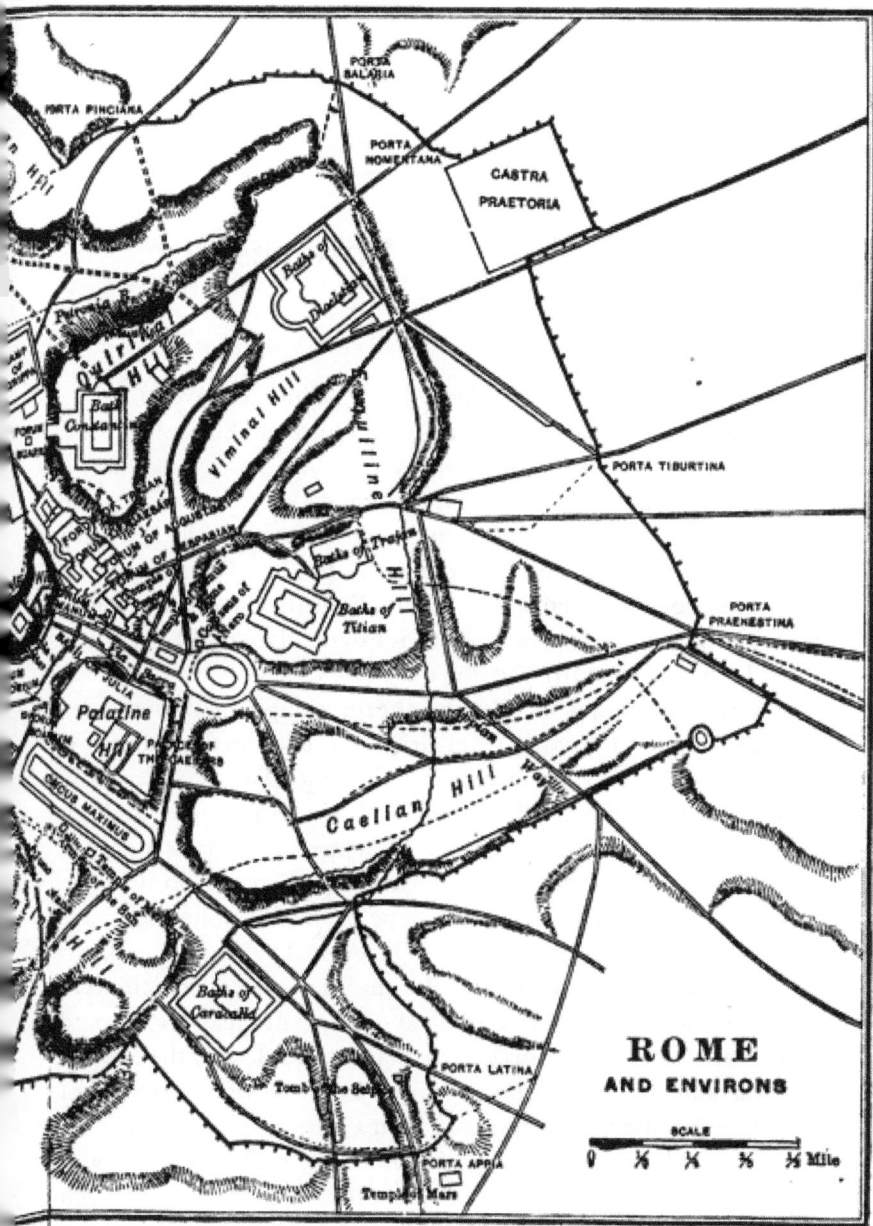

PORTA
SALARIA

PORTA PINCIANA

PORTA
NOMENTANA

CASTRA
PRAETORIA

Baths of
Diocletian

Porta Salaria

Quirinal Hill

Viminal HILL

Baths of
Constantine

FORUM OF TRAJAN
FORUM OF AUGUSTUS
FORUM OF NERVA
FORUM OF VESPASIAN

Esquiline Hill

PORTA TIBURTINA

Baths of Trajan

Baths of
Titus

Column of
Trajan

PORTA
PRAENESTINA

Palatine

PALACE OF
THE CAESARS

Caelian HILL

Old Wall

CIRCUS MAXIMUS

Baths of
Caracalla

Tomb of the Scipios

PORTA LATINA

ROME
AND ENVIRONS

PORTA APPIA

Temple of Mars

SCALE

0   ⅛   ¼   ⅜   ½ Mile

CHAPTER 47

Public Buildings, Squares, etc.

Rome was built on seven hills,—the Palatine, the Aventine, the Capitoline, the Esquiline (the largest), the Quirínal, the Viminal, and the Coelian.

There were various public squares (*forum* = square or park). Some were places of resort for public business, and most were adorned with *porticos*. The most celebrated square was the **Forum Románum**, or simply **The Forum**. There were also the **Forum Caesaris** and **Forum Trajáni**. Some served as markets; as **Forum Boarium**, the cattle market; **Forum Suarium**, the hog market, etc.

Temples were numerous. The **Pantheon** (temple of all the gods), built by Agrippa and restored by Hadrian, was dedicated to Jupiter. It was situated outside of the city, in the Campus Martius, and is now used as a Christian church. The Temple of Apollo Palatínus, built by Augustus, was on the Palatine Hill. It contained a library, which was founded by Augustus. The Temple of Aesculapius was on an island in the Tiber; that of Concordia, on the slope of the Capitoline Hill, was dedicated in 377 b.c. and restored by Tiberius. The Temple of Janus was an arched passage east of the Forum, the gates of which were open during war. Up to the time of Ovid the gates had been closed but three times, once in Numa's reign, again at the close of the Second Punic War, and after the battle of Actium. Janus was one of the oldest Latin divinities, and was represented with a face in front and another on the back of his head. From him is named the month of January.

There were several temples of Jupiter, the most famous of which was that of Jupiter Optimus, Maximus, or Capitolínus, built during the dynasty of the Tarquins, and splendidly adorned. (See Chapter 5) There were also numerous temples of Juno, of Mars, and of other *deities*.

The **Colosséum** was the largest building in Rome. (See Chapter 46.)

There were three theatres; that of Pompey (see Chapter 46.), of Marcellus, and of Balbus; and several circuses, the most famous of which was the Circus Maximus. (See Chapter 46.)

The **Basilicae** were halls of justice (court-houses). The most important was the Basilica Julia, begun by Caesar and finished by Augustus, which was situated on the south side of the Forum, and the foundations of which can still be seen.

The **Curia**, or Senate-house, was in the *Forum*. Each of the thirty *curiae* had a place of meeting, called also a *curia*, where were discussed public questions pertaining to politics, finance, or religion.

The **Public Baths** were numerous. There were *Thermae* (hot baths) of Nero, of Titus, of Trajan, of Caracalla, and of others, ruins of which still exist.

Pure water was brought into the city from the surrounding hills by fourteen different aqueducts, all of which were well built, and three of which are still in use. The first aqueduct (*Aqua Appia*) was built about 313 b.c. by Appius Claudius.

Sewers intersected Rome in all directions, and some were of immense size. The **Cloáca Maxima**, built by Tarquin, was the largest, and is still in use. Its innermost arch has a diameter of fourteen feet.

There are said to have been twenty **Triumphal Arches**, of which five now remain:

1. The **Arch of Drusus**, on the Appian Way, erected in honour of Claudius Drusus.

2. The **Arch of Titus,** at the foot of the Palatine Hill, built by Titus to commemorate his conquest of Judaea. The *bas-reliefs* on this arch represent the spoils taken from the temple at Jerusalem, carried in triumphal procession.

3. The **Arch of Septimius Séverus**, built by the Senate in 207 *a. d.,* at the end of the Via Sacra, in honour of the Emperor and his two sons for their conquest of the Parthians and Arabians.

4. The **Arch of Galliénus**.

5. The **Arch of Constantine**.

There were two famous **Mausoléa**; that of Augustus, now in ruins, and that of Hadrian, which, stripped of its ornaments, is now the Castle of San Angelo.

The Columns commemorating persons or events were numerous.

The most remarkable of these were erected for naval victories, and called **Columnae Rostrátae**. The one of Duilius, in honour of the victory at Mylae (261 b. c), still stands. It has three ship-beaks attached to each side. Columns were built in honour of several Emperors. That of Trajan is perhaps best known.

The **Columna Milliaria** was a milestone set up by Augustus in the Forum, from which all distances on the different public roads were measured. It was called **Milliarium Aureum**, or the golden milestone.

CHAPTER 48

Colonies—The Calendar—Religion

Colonies were established by Rome throughout its whole history. They were intended to keep in check a conquered people, and also to repress hostile incursions. Many were founded to provide for veteran soldiers; a practice which was begun by Sulla, and continued under the Emperors.

No colony was established without a *lex*, *plebiscitum*, or *senatus consultum*. Religious ceremonies always accompanied their foundation, and the anniversary was observed.

The colonies were divided into two classes, *viz*. Roman, and Latin or military. Members of the former class had all the rights of Roman citizens; those of the latter could not vote in the *Comitia* at Rome. The *Latini*, who were once Roman citizens, and who always felt equal to them, were uneasy in their subordinate position. But by the Julian law, passed in 90 b. c, they acquired the right of voting at Rome, and were placed on the same footing as Roman colonists.

THE CALENDAR.

The Roman year began with March. There were twelve months, and each month had three divisions, the **Kalends**, **Nones**, and **Ides**. The *Kalends* fell on the first of the month; the *Nones*, on the 7th of March, May, July, and October; in other months, on the 5th. The *Ides* came eight days after the *Nones*. If an event happened on these divisions, it was said to occur on the *Kalends*, *Nones*, or *Ides* of the month. If it happened between any of these divisions, it was said to occur so many days *before* the division *following* the event The year was reckoned from the foundation of the city (753 b. c.), and often the names of the Consuls of that year were added.

197

RELIGION.

The Romans were religious, and had numerous gods and goddesses: **Jupiter** and **Juno**, the god and goddess of light; **Saturn**, the god of seed-sowing; **Tellus**, the goddess of the nourishing earth; **Ceres**, the goddess of growth; **Consus** and **Ops**, who presided over the harvest; **Pales**, the god of the flocks; and **Lupercus**, the god of fertility. Various festivals were celebrated in honour of these, as the Saturnalia, in December; the *Tellilia* (Tellus), *Cerialia* (Ceres), and *Palilia* (Pales), in April; and the *Lupercalia*, in February.

Vesta was the goddess of the house, and as every family had an altar erected for her worship, so the state, as a combination of families, had a common altar to her in the temple of Vesta. In this temple were also worshipped the Penátes and Lares.

The **Lares** were special guardians of private houses. Some protected fields and cities. Images of Lares of diminutive size, clad often in dog-skins, were ranged along the hearth. The people honoured them on the *Kalends* of May and other festival days by decking them with flowers, and by offering them wine, incense, flour, and portions of their meals upon plates.

The **Penátes** were kept and worshipped only in the inmost chambers of houses and temples. Their statues, made of wax, wood, or ivory, were also kept in the inner hall.

The priestesses of Vesta were six in number, and were called **Vestal Virgins**. When a vestal was to be elected, the *Pontifex Maximus* chose twenty young girls from high families. Of these one was chosen by lot to fill the vacancy, and she was bound to serve for thirty years. The Vestals were preceded by a *lictor* when in public. They had private seats in the public shows, and had the power of delivering from punishment any condemned person they happened to meet. They wore white dresses and white fillets. Their chief duty was to keep the fire always burning on the hearth (*focus publicus*) in the temple. They could not marry.

FLAMINES.

The **Flamines** were priests devoted to the service of some particular god. There were fifteen, and they were chosen first in the *Comitia Curiáta*, and afterwards probably in the Tribúta. The most distinguished of all the *Flamines* was the *Flamen Diális* (Jupiter). He had the right to a *lictor*, to the *sella curúlis*, and to a seat in the Senate. If one in bonds took refuge in his house, the chains were at once removed.

This priest, however, could not be away from the city a single night, and was forbidden to sleep out of his own bed for three consecutive nights. He was not allowed to mount a horse, or even to touch one, or to look upon an army outside of the city walls.

THE SALII.

These were priests of Mars, twelve in number, and always chosen from the patricians. They celebrated the festival of Mars on the 1st of March, and for several successive days.

THE AUGURES.

This body varied in number, from three, in early times, to sixteen in the time of Caesar. It was composed of men who were believed to interpret the will of the gods, and to declare whether the omens were favourable or otherwise. No public act of any kind could be performed, no election held, no law passed, no war waged, without first consulting the omens. There was no appeal from the decision of the Augurs, and hence their power was great. They held office for life, and were a close corporation, filling their own vacancies until 103 b.c.

THE FETIALES.

This was another body of priests holding office for life, and numbering probably twenty. They were expected, whenever any dispute arose with other nations, to demand satisfaction, to determine whether hostilities should be begun, and to preside at any ratification of peace.

CHAPTER 49

The Roman Army in Caesar's Time

The **Legio** was composed of infantry, and, though larger, corresponded to our regiment. It was divided into ten *cohorts* (battalions), each *cohort* into three maniples (companies), and each *maniple* into two *centuries* (platoons). In theory the number in each legion was six thousand, in practice about four thousand. The usual order of battle was to draw up each legion in three lines (*acies triplex*), the first consisting of four *cohorts*, the second and third of three each.

The defensive armour of the legionary soldier was a helmet of metal or leather, a shield (four feet by two and a half), greaves, and corselets of various material. The outer garment was a woollen blanket, fastened to the shoulders by a buckle. Higher officers wore a long purple cloak.

The offensive armour was a short, straight two-edged sword (*gladius*), about two feet long, worn by privates on the right side, so as not to interfere with the shield, but on the left side by officers. The javelin (*pilum*) was a heavy wooden shaft with an iron head, the whole about seven feet long and weighing fully ten pounds. [1]

All legionary soldiers were Roman citizens. The auxiliaries were hired or drafted troops, and were always light-armed The cavalry in Caesar's time was made up of auxiliaries taken from the different provinces.

The officers were:—

1. The **Imperator**, or commander in chief.

2. The **Legáti**, or staff officers, varying in number. Caesar had

---

1. *The Military System of the Romans* by Albert Harkness, *The Auxilia of the Roman Imperial Army* by G. L. Cheeseman and *Caesar's Army* by Harry Pratt Judson also published by Leonaur.

ten.

3. The **Quaestor**, or quartermaster.

4. The **Tribtúni Militum**, numbering six in each legion, and assisting the *Imperator* in his duties.

5. The **Praefecti**, who held various subordinate commands.

6. The **Centuriónes**, who were non-commissioned officers, and rose in rank for good service. There were sixty *centurions* in each legion, six in each *cohort*, and one in each *century*. They were promoted from the ranks, but rarely rose above centurion of the first rank. All the officers, except the *centurions*, came from either senatorial or equestrian families.

The **Conors Praetoria** was a body of picked troops that acted as body guard to the *Imperator*.

The **Standard** (*signum*) of the legion was an eagle with out-stretched wings, perched upon a pole.

The Romans when on the march fortified their camp every night. They made it rectangular in shape, and threw up fortifications always in the same way. It was surrounded by a ditch and rampart. The legionary soldiers encamped next to the wall on the inside of the fortifications, thus surrounding the cavalry, the auxiliaries, the general and his staff. The general's tent was called the **Praetorium**, and the entrance to the camp in front of his tent was called the Praetorian Gate. The opposite entrance was called the Decuman Gate.

CHAPTER 50

Legendary Rome

Aeneas, son of Anchises and Venus, fled from Troy after its capture by the Greeks (1184?) and came to Italy. He was accompanied by his son **Iúlus**, and a number of brave followers. **Latínus**, who was king of the district where Aeneas landed, received him kindly, and gave him his daughter, **Lavinia**, in marriage. Aeneas founded a city, which he named **Lavinium**, in honour of his wife. After his death, Iúlus, also called **Ascanius**, became king. He founded on Mount Albánus a city, which he called **Alba Longa**, and to it transferred the capital.

Here a number of kings ruled in succession, the last of whom was **Silvius Procas**, who left two sons, **Numitor**, the older, and **Amulius**. They divided the kingdom, the former choosing the property, the latter the crown. Numitor had two children, a son and a daughter. Amulius, fearing that they might aspire to the throne, murdered the son, and made the daughter, **Rhea Silvia**, a Vestal virgin. This he did to prevent her marrying, for this was forbidden to Vestal virgins. She, however, became pregnant by Mars, and had twin sons, whom she named **Romulus** and **Remus**. When Amulius was informed of this, he cast their mother into prison, and ordered the boys to be drowned in the Tiber,

At this time the river was swollen by rains, and had overflowed its banks. The boys were thrown into a shallow place, escaped drowning, and, the water subsiding, they were left on dry land. A she wolf, hearing their cries, ran to them and suckled them. **Faustulus**, a shepherd who was nearby, seeing this, took the boys home and reared them. When they grew up and learned who they were, they killed Amulius, and gave the kingdom to their grandfather, Numitor. Then (753) they founded a city on Mount Palatínus, which they called **Rome**, after Romulus. While they were building a wall around this city, Remus was killed in a quarrel with his brother.

Romulus, first king of Rome, ruled for thirty-seven years (753-716). He found the city needed inhabitants, and to increase their number he opened an asylum, to which many refugees fled. But wives were needed. To supply this want, he celebrated games, and invited the neighbouring people, the **Sabines**, to attend the sports. When all were engaged in looking on, the Romans suddenly made a rush and seized the Sabine virgins. This bold robbery caused a war, which finally ended in a compromise, and a sharing of the city with the Sabines. Romulus then chose one hundred Senators, whom he called **Patres**. He also divided the people into thirty wards. In the thirty-seventh year of his reign he disappeared, and was believed to have been taken up into heaven.

One year followed without any king, and then **Numa Pompilius** (716-673), a Sabine from Cures, was chosen. He was a good man, and a great lawgiver. Many sacred rites were instituted by him to civilize his barbarous subjects. He reformed the calendar, and built a temple to the god Janus. **Tullus Hostilius** (673-641) succeeded him. His reign was noted for the fall of Alba Longa. Then came **Ancus Marcius** (640-616), the grandson of Numa. He was a good ruler and popular. He conquered the Latins, enlarged the city, and built new walls around it. He was the first to build a prison, and to bridge the Tiber.[1] He also founded a city at its mouth, which he called Ostia.

The next three kings were of Etruscan origin. **Lucius Tarquinius Priscus** (616-578) went to Rome first during the reign of Ancus, and, becoming a favourite of his, was appointed guardian of his sons. After the death of Ancus, he wrested the government from them, and became king himself. He increased the Senators to two hundred, carried on many wars successfully, and thus enlarged the territory of the city. He built the **Cloáca Maxima**, or great sewer, which is used today. Tarquin also began the temple of **Jupiter Capitolínus**, on the Capitoline Hill. He was killed in the thirty-eighth year of his reign by the sons of Ancus, from whom he had snatched the kingdom.

His successor was his son-in-law, **Servius Tullius** (578- 534), who enlarged the city still more, built a temple to Diána, and took a census of the people. It was found that the city and suburbs contained 83,000 souls. Servius was killed by his daughter, Tullia, and her husband, Tarquinius Superbus, son of Priscus.

---

1. This bridge was called the *pons sublicius, i. e.* a bridge resting on piles.

Tarquinius Superbus succeeded to the throne (534– 510). He was energetic in war, and conquered many neighbouring places, among which was Ardea, a city of the Rutuli. He finished the temple of Jupiter, begun by his father. He also obtained the **Sibylline Books**. A woman from Cumae, a Greek colony, came to him, and offered for sale nine books of oracles and prophecies; but the price seemed exorbitant, and he refused to purchase them. The sibyl then burned three, and, returning, asked the same price for the remaining six. The king again refused. She burned three more, and obtained from the monarch for her last three the original price. These books were preserved in the Capitol, and held in great respect. They were destroyed with the temple by fire, on July 6, 83. Two men had charge of them, who were called *duoviri sacrórum*. The worship of the Greek *deities*, Apollo and Latóna, among others, was introduced through these books.

In 510 a conspiracy was formed against Tarquin by **Brutus, Collatínus**, and others, and the gates of the city were closed against him. [2] A Republic was then formed, with two Consuls at the head of the government.

Tarquin made three attempts to recover his power at Rome, all unsuccessful.[3] In the last attempt (508), he was assisted by **Porsena**, king of the Etruscans. They advanced against the city from the north. **Horatius Cocles**, a brave young man, alone defended the bridge (*pons sublicius*) over the Tiber until it was torn down behind him. He then swam the river in safety to his friends. [4]

During the siege of the city, **Quintus Mucius Scaevola**, a courageous youth, stole into the camp of the enemy with the intention of killing King Porsena, but by mistake killed his secretary instead. He was seized and carried to Porsena, who tried to frighten him by threats of burning. Instead of replying, Scaevola held his right hand on the burning altar until it was consumed. The king, admiring this heroic act, pardoned him. Out of gratitude, Scaevola told the king that three hundred other men as brave as himself had sworn to kill him. Porsena was so alarmed, that he made peace, and withdrew from the city. Mucius received his name Scaevola (left-handed) on account of

---

2. The cause of the conspiracy was the violence offered by Sextus, Tarquin's son, to Lucretia, wife of Collatínus. Unable to bear the humiliation, she killed herself in the presence of her family, having first appealed to them to avenge her wrongs .
3. The victory of Lake Regillus, which has been painted by Macaulay in glowing colours, was gained over Tarquin in 509.
4. See Macaulay's *Lays of Ancient Rome*.

this loss of his right hand.

Tarquin went to Tusculum, where he spent the rest of his days in retirement.

In 494 the plebeians at Rome rebelled, because they were exhausted by taxes and military service. A large part of them left the city, and crossed the Anio to a mountain (Mons Sacer) nearby. The Senate sent **Menenius Agrippa** to treat with them. By his exertions [5] the people were induced to return to the city, and for the first time were allowed to have officers chosen from their own ranks to represent their interests. These officers were called *Tribúni Plebis*.

Two years later (492) Gaius Marcius, one of the patricians, met and defeated the Volsci, a neighbouring tribe, at **Corioli**. For this he received the name of **Coriolánus**. During a famine, he advised that grain should not be distributed to the plebeians unless they relinquished their right to choose the *Tribúni Plebis*. For this he was banished. Having obtained command of a Volscian army, he marched against Rome, and came within five miles of the city. Here he was met by a deputation of his own citizens, who begged him to spare the city. He refused; but, when his wife and mother added their tears, he was induced to withdraw the army. He was afterwards killed by the Volscians as a traitor. [6]

After the expulsion of Tarquin, the **Fabii** were among the most distinguished men at Rome. There were three brothers, and for seven consecutive years one of them was Consul. It looked as if the Fabian *gens* would get control of the government. The state took alarm, and the whole gens, numbering 306 males and 4,000 dependents, was driven from Rome. For two years they carried on war alone against the Veientes, but finally were surprised and slain (477). One boy, Quintus Fabius Vibulánus, alone survived to preserve the name and *gens* of the Fabii.

In 458 the Romans were hard pressed by the Aequi. Their territory had been overrun, and their Consuls, cut off in some defiles, were in imminent danger of destruction. Lucius **Quinctius Cincinnátus** was appointed Dictator. He was one of the most noted Roman warriors of this period. The ambassadors sent to inform him of his appointment found him working with bare arms in his field. Cincinnatus told his wife to throw over him his mantle, that he might receive the

---

5. Menenius is said to have related for them the famous fable of the belly and members.

6. See Shakespeare's *Coriolanus*.

messengers of the state with proper respect. Such was the simplicity of his character, and yet so deeply did he reverence authority. The Aequi could not withstand his vigorous campaign, but were obliged soon to surrender, and made to pass under the yoke as a sign of humiliation. The Dictator enjoyed a well earned triumph.

In 451 one of the *Decemviri*, **Appius Claudius**, was captivated by the beauty of a patrician maiden, **Virginia**,[7] a daughter of Lucius Virginius, and the betrothed of Lucius Icilius. He formed, with one of his tools, an infamous plot to obtain possession of Virginia, under pretence that she was a slave. When, in spite of all the efforts of the girl's father and lover, the *Decemvir* had, in his official capacity, adjudged her to be the slave of his tool, Virginius plunged a knife into his daughter's bosom, in presence of the people in the *Forum*. The enraged populace compelled the *Decemviri* to resign, and Appius, to escape worse punishment, put an end to his own life.

Marcus Furius Camillus was a famous man of a little later period. He was called a second Romulus for his distinguished services. In 396 he captured Veii, after a siege of ten years. On his return he celebrated the most magnificent triumph yet seen at Rome. He was afterwards impeached for not having fairly divided the spoils obtained at Veii, and went into exile at Ardea. When Rome was besieged by the Gauls under Brennus, in 390, Camillus was recalled and made Dictator. At the head of forty thousand men he hastened to the city, raised the siege, and in the battle which followed annihilated the Gauls. He was Dictator five times, Interrex three times, Military Tribune twice, and enjoyed four triumphs. He died at the advanced age of eighty-eight.

Brennus was the famous leader of the Senones, a tribe of Gauls, who invaded Italy about 390. He defeated the Romans at the River Allia (July 18, 390), and captured the city, except the Capitol, which he besieged for six months. During the siege he tried to surprise the garrison, but was repulsed by Manlius, who was awakened by the cackling of some geese. Peace was finally purchased by the Romans by the payment of a thousand pounds of gold. To increase the weight, Brennus is said to have thrown his sword on the scales. At this juncture, as the story runs, Camillus appeared with his troops, ordered the gold to be removed, saying that Rome must be ransomed with steel, and not gold. In the battle which followed, the Gauls were defeated.

---

7. See Macaulay's *Lays of Ancient Rome*.

Chronology

B. C. 753 Foundation of Rome by Romulus.

753-510 Regal Period.

753-716. Romulus.

716-673. Numa Pompilius.

673-641. Tullus Hostilius.

640-616. Ancus Marcius.

616-578. Tarquinius Priscus.

578-534. Servius Tullius.

534-510 Tarquinius Superbus.

510-30 The Republic.

509. Battle of Lake Regillus.

508. Porsena. Horatius Cocles.

494. Tribúni Plebis. Menenius Agrippa.

492. Corioli. Coriolánus.

477 Destruction of the Fabian *Gens*.

458 War with the Aequians. Cincinnátus.

451 The *Decemviri*. Appius Claudius. Virginia.

396. Capture of Veii. Camillus.

390 Siege of Rome by Brennus. Battle at the Allia River (July 18).

387. The planting of the first military or Latin colonies.

367. The Licinian Rogations.

353 Caere: the first Municipium.

343-341 First Samnite War.

340-338. The Latin War.

338. Antium, the first Roman or maritime colony.

326-304. The Second Samnite War.

321. The Caudine Forks.

298-290. The Third Samnite War.

295 Sentinum.

283. Lake Vadimónis.

281-272. Pyrrhus.

280. Heracléa. Cineas.

279. Asculum.

274. Beneventum.

272. Rome mistress of Italy; morality at its height

264. Period of foreign conquest begins.

264-241. First Punic War.

260. Lipara; Mylae.

257 Tyndaris.

256. Ecnomus. Regulus at Clupea.

249. Drepana.

241. Aegates Insulae. Catulus. Hamilcar Barca.

237 Sardinia and Corsica acquired, and provincial system established.

229. Illyrican War. Important results.

222. Gallia Cisalpína acquired by battle of Telamon.

220. Hannibal in Spain.

219. Saguntum.

218-202. Second Punic War. Ticínus. Trebia.

217. Trasiménus. Casilínum.

216. Cannae.

212. Capture of Syracuse. Archimedes.

207. Baecula. Metaurus.

202. Zama.

214-205. First Macedonian War.

200-197. Second Macedonian War.

198. Cynoscephalae.

190 Magnesia.

183. Death of Africánus, Hannibal, and Philopoemen.

171-168. Third Macedonian War.

168. Pydna.

149-146. ThirdPunic War.

149. Death of Cato the elder.

146. Destruction of Carthage and Corinth.

143-133 The Numantine War.

134-132. The Servile War.

133 Tiberius Gracchus.

129. Death of Africánus the younger.

123-121. Gaius Gracchus.

118-104. The Jugurthine War. Metellus. Marius. Sulla.

102. Aquae Sextiae.

101. Vercellae.

90-89. The Italian or Social War.

86. Death of Marius.

86-84. Sulla's campaign against Mithradátes.

84. Death of Cinna.

80. Reforms of Sulla.

78. Death of Sulla.

80-72. Sertorius in Spain.

73-71. Spartacus.

72-67. Campaign of Lucullus against Mithradátes.

67. Pompey conquers the pirates.

67-61. Pompey in the East.

63. Cicero Consul. Catiline.

59. First Triumvirate formed. Caesar's first Consulship. The Leges Juliae. Clodius. Cicero's banishment. Cato sent to Cyprus.

58-49. Caesar in Gaul.

57. Recall of Cicero. Return of Cato.

53. Death of Crassus.

52. Murder of Clodius. Pompey's consulship and separation from Caesar.

49. Caesar crosses the Rubicon. Siege and capture of Ilerda.

48 (Jan. 4) Caesar sails from Brundisium. Victory of Pompey near the sea-board. (Aug. 9) Pharsalia. (Sept. 28) Murder of Pompey.

47. Caesar establishes Cleopátra on the throne of Egypt. Battle of Zela. (Sept.) Caesar returns to Rome.

46 (Apr. 4) Thapsus. Death of Cato the younger.

45 (Mar. 17) Munda.

44 (Mar. 15) Murder of Caesar.

43 (Nov. 27) The Second Triumvirate. (Dec.) Murder of Cicero.

42 (Nov.) Philippi.

36. Naulochus.

31 (Sept. 2) Actium.

THE EMPIRE.

B.C. A.D.

30-41. The Julian Emperors.

30-14. Augustus.

A.D.

14-37 Tiberius.

37-41 Caligula.

41-68. The Claudian Emperors.

41-54 Claudius.

54-68. Nero.

68-69. Galba.

69. Otho.

69-96. The Flavian Emperors.

69-79. Vespasian.

79. Destruction of Jerusalem.

79-81. Titus.

80. Destruction of Herculaneum and Pompeii,

81-96. Domitian.

96-180. The Five Good Emperors.

96-98. Nerva.

98-117. Trajan. Limit of Empire reached.

117-138. Hadrian.

138-161. Antoninus Pius.

161-180. Marcus Aurelius.

180-192. Commodus.

192-284. From Pertinax to Diocletian.

284-305. Diocletian.

306-37. Constantine the Great.

312. Edict of Milan.

325. Council of Nice.

337-476. From Constantine to Romulus Augustulus.